Ephraim Brown House, North Bloomfield. Built in 1815-16

Early Homes of Ohio

By I. T. FRARY

DOVER PUBLICATIONS, INC.
NEW YORK

Published in Canada by General Publishing Company, Ltd., 30 Lesmill Road, Don Mills, Toronto, Ontario.

Published in the United Kingdom by Constable and Company, Ltd., 10 Orange Street, London WC 2.

This Dover edition, first published in 1970, is an unabridged republication of the work originally published by Garrett & Massie, Inc., Richmond, Va. in 1936. The publisher is grateful to the East Cleveland Public Library for making a copy of the book available for reproduction.

Standard Book Number: 486-22619-0
Library of Congress Catalog Card Number: 76-110298

Manufactured in the United States of America
Dover Publications, Inc.
180 Varick Street
New York, N.Y. 10014

CONTENTS

CONTENTS

PLATES

PLATES

PLATES

ix

PLATES

PLATES

PLATES

xii

INTRODUCTION

THE compilation of material for this book began with the casual photographing of old houses and doorways as a byproduct of outings in the family automobile. Once introduced to the early homes of Ohio, a growing interest was aroused in the achievements of the pioneer builders, together with a desire to preserve a somewhat comprehensive photographic record of the old buildings which were rapidly disappearing or losing their original appearance through fire, decay, vandalism, remodeling, and other destructive agencies of man and nature.

The amazing variety and quality of design and workmanship in these old buildings revealed a hitherto unappreciated and unwritten chapter in our state's history, and a natural curiosity was aroused to learn something of the men who designed and built these structures, and of the men and women for whose lives they formed a background.

Such information is secured with great difficulty. Family tradition is notoriously inaccurate, and historians are almost wholly unconcerned as to the achievements of architects and builders. Family tradition is amply satisfied if an article belonged to a certain deceased relative and is "over a hundred years old." Historians are apparently thrilled only with the doings of soldiers, lawyers, ministers, and doctors.

Then, too, the descendants of the pioneers seem to have inherited the wanderlust that lured their ancestors away from the settled regions of the Atlantic States and sent them plodding through the forests to the Ohio Country. So I found that great numbers of the old houses have long since been deserted by the original families, and are now occupied by strangers, often of foreign birth, to whom the old names and the old traditions mean nothing. Occupants of my own grandfather's farm were unfamiliar with the family name when I asked permission to photograph the house.

As most of the photographing of these old places has been done during holidays and vacations, little attempt was made to secure any but photographic records, it being hoped that others would volunteer to do the work of research and writing.

Enough data were gathered, however, to make possible an illustrated lecture which was called "Early Homes of Ohio." The demand for this lecture has been so persistent (it has been given one hundred times in ten years), and so many inquiries have been made for the information which it contains that I finally determined to put it in book form. The material accumulated in this undertaking made the text of the lecture alone seem so inadequate that it was finally decided to use this as Part I of a book that should cover the subject with some degree of thoroughness.

The most difficult feature of the work has been that of securing adequate information regarding the early designers and builders. Records of innumerable carpenters, builders, and masons were discovered but with scant distinction made between those possessing some degree of architectural training and those who were mere workmen. Few could be ranked as architects, but many merited the title of master builder.

The first noteworthy discovery in this field consisted of the original plans and bills of materials for the Effinger House at Lancaster. These were in the possession of Mrs. Adaline E. Webb, granddaughter of the original owner and are now in the possession of the Columbus Gallery of Fine Arts. Next came a manuscript, in the possession of Mrs. Henry Farwell of Hudson, which embodied very complete information regarding the life of her grandfather, Colonel Lemuel Porter and his son, Simeon Porter. The trail of Jonathan Goldsmith was followed rather casually for several years, when an intensive effort resulted in unearthing another manuscript written by Goldsmith's daughter, Lucia Jones Goldsmith. This was generously lent by Frank Goldsmith Johnson, a grandson of Goldsmith, who also furnished much additional information. A granddaughter, Mrs. Abigail Goldsmith Haver, turned over a veritable treasure in the form of original drawings and specifications by Goldsmith, the most important documentary evidence thus far discovered. No trace of Goldsmith's fine library has been discovered.

Another paper, prepared by W. Dominick Benes and read on February 14, 1928, before the Cleveland Chapter, American Institute of Architects, added a dramatic climax to the Porter and Goldsmith records by showing that Simeon Porter and Goldsmith's pupil and son-in-law, Charles W. Heard, ultimately became partners and practiced architecture for many years in Cleveland.

Evidence, to be found everywhere, points to the common use by Ohio builders of handbooks published by Asher Benjamin, Minard Lafever, and others, but only as my manuscript was well under way was the discovery made of a copy of Benjamin's *The Practical House Carpenter* (1830) in the home that Burritt Blakeslee built for himself near Medina. Details of work executed by him give convincing evidence of his study of this book. Opportunity for studying the book, the house, and examples of Blakeslee's work was generously afforded by his daughter-in-law, Mrs. Edwin C. Blakeslee, and his granddaughter, Miss Mary Blakeslee.

Copies of books by both Benjamin and Lafever, in my library, have made it possible to check details of existing buildings back to plates of design from which they were doubtless taken.

The story of Joseph Barker was pieced together by Charles E. Patton, while searching for material on the early builders of Marietta, to be used in a thesis submitted for his Master's degree, at Western Reserve University. Through his courtesy this information was made available for use here.

An item of unusual interest and importance was the set of builder's contracts, drawn up in 1834 by Henry B. Curtis, that was made available by his grandson, Henry C. Devin of Mount Vernon. In these contracts reference is made to plates in *Shaw's Architecture,* photographs from which, together with information regarding the book, were secured through the generous coöperation of Dr. Leicester B. Holland and Miss Natalie G. Plunkett of the Library of Congress.

Thanks are also due Rhea Mansfield Knittle for encouragement in the prosecution of this work and for the gift of data gathered by her while engaged in a search for material of a kindred nature.

Innumerable owners and occupants of houses and other buildings have made it possible, through their kindness and courtesy, to build up the large collection of photographs from which the illustrations for this book have been chosen. Many also have coöperated by searching out data that proved of inestimable value in rounding out this story of the past. It is a matter of deep regret that each can not be thanked here individually.

Evidence of the widespread interest in our country's early architecture is found in a handbook on *Historic House Museums* by Laurence Vail Coleman, Director of the American Association of Museums. In it are listed some four hundred old structures that are being preserved as museums or as historic monuments, and nearly as many more have been brought to Mr. Coleman's attention since the book was published.

Records of early American architecture are being assembled by the Division of Fine Arts of the Library of Congress in a collection of photographic negatives and prints, and of drawings, which is listed as the Pictorial Archives of Early American Architecture. This collection was augmented in 1934 by thousands of drawings and photographs secured by the Historic American Buildings Survey, and it is planned to continue making such records under the joint auspices of the Library of Congress, the National Park Service, and the American Institute of Architects.

Various societies throughout the country are devoting much time and money to the preservation of historic buildings, our own Ohio State Archaeological and Historical Society having made an excellent beginning under the direction of Henry C. Shetrone. The restoration of Schoenbrunn, the enclosing of the Rufus Putnam House at Marietta under the roof of the Campus Martius Museum, and the acquisition of the so-called "King's Palace" at Zoar are among the notable achievements of the society, by means of which Ohio history is being made vital through concrete illustrations of its pioneer life.

We Americans are just beginning to appreciate the importance of our comparatively brief history and with appreciation are realizing the value of our early architecture as source material in the study of that history. European nations have long cherished the architecture and art of their past, and it is to be hoped that we will follow more assiduously the lead of countries across the sea by preserving as historic monuments surviving structures which tell far more vividly than words the story of our past. The photographs reproduced here afford indisputable evidence that Ohio's early homes tell a worthy story, and that many are richly deserving of preservation.

I. T. FRARY.

The Cleveland Museum of Art
January, 1936.

PLATE I: *Ohio Land Company's Office, Marietta. Built in 1788*

PART I: EARLY HOMES OF OHIO

WHATEVER monuments people may leave behind, none give such intimate and accurate evidence of their character as do the homes in which they lived. The dwellings excavated at Pompeii bring us closer to the Roman people than does their literature. The palace of Versailles tells us more vividly the causes of the French Revolution than do the pages of Carlyle's *History*. Throughout the world today agencies are at work preserving dwellings of all kinds, cottages, castles, and palaces, that coming generations may see, with their own eyes, actual homes which reflect the manners, taste, and character of individuals, nations, and epochs of the past.

In our own country numerous old houses are being preserved, by families, governmental agencies, or patriotic societies, as memorials to our past, and as textbooks from which we may gain closer acquaintance with our forefathers, and understand more clearly their characters and their mode of living.

Ohio has her share of such landmarks, but she has been rather modest in proclaiming them, in fact the older states bordering the Atlantic have been so prone to accept credit for everything worth while pertaining to our country's youthful years, that we of the middle west have meekly assented, and accepted a minor part in the pageant of America.

We find, however, that Ohio has a most colorful, romantic, and vital history, the pages of which are illustrated by existing houses, churches, and public buildings of fine quality that bring us close to the characters who moved through the chapters of its past.

Ohio may well be called the melting pot of America, for here came immigrants from all the eastern states, bringing with them the customs, habits, and ideals of their former homes and, uncon-

[1]

PLATE 2: *Headley Inn, on National Road near Zanesville. Built in 1802 and 1833*

sciously perhaps, reproducing in the wilderness of the Ohio Country the manner of life to which they had been accustomed in the
east.

And so, if you are familiar with the early architecture of the thirteen original colonies or states, you can determine pretty accurately
the origin of the early settlers in almost any old Ohio town by
studying the character of buildings which survive them, and comparing these with their eastern prototypes. Thus that portion of
Ohio that was fed from the National Road and the Ohio River,
drew its settlers largely from Pennsylvania, Maryland, Virginia,
and the more southerly states. Here we find architecture largely
of the types common there. On the other hand, the northern portion of the state was settled mostly by people from New England,
who came across New York state and along the southern shore of
Lake Erie.

All through the counties adjacent to the lake, especially those
that comprise what is still known as the Western Reserve and the
Firelands, we find buildings that are counterparts of those in the
New England States. Apparently contradicting this general statement are the old Painesville (Plate 9) and Unionville Taverns,
built shortly after the War of 1812, which are much in the style of
Mount Vernon. The explanation of this is obvious; Washington
being the outstanding personage of his time, and his home one of
distinctive design, anyone, anywhere in the country might quite
naturally turn to it for suggestion when planning a building of
importance. Then, of course, these currents of immigration eddied
and flowed together, so the New England types of architecture are
on occasion to be found in southern Ohio, and those of the South
in the lake regions.

Most of the old buildings were comparatively simple, the interest on the exterior being concentrated largely about the doorways,
which show a surprising diversity of design.

Before looking at the buildings themselves, it may be well to

PLATE 3: *Headley Inn—Room on second floor. Ceiling beams are black walnut. Stairway runs from kitchen in basement to attic*

[4]

PLATE 4: *Headley Inn—Stairway. Decorations painted in colors on risers, stringers, and baseboard of second story rooms*

PLATE 5: *Headley Inn—Bedroom mantel. Painted black and white. Polychrome decoration painted on baseboard*

glance back for a moment at Ohio's historical background. Up to the time of the Revolutionary War, the Ohio Country had been a wilderness inhabited by a comparatively small number of Indians, with here and there an adventurous trapper or trader. Following the Revolution, these western lands were ceded to the government by the various states, certain tracts being reserved for special purposes. One of these tracts of over 2,800,000 acres in extent, bordered the southern shore of Lake Erie from the Pennsylvania line west 120 miles. This was reserved by the State of Connecticut, and sold to realize endowment for her public schools. It is still known as the Western Reserve. To the west of this, an area of 500,000 acres, known as the Firelands, was retained to indemnify citizens of Connecticut whose property had been burned by the British. In the southern part of the state, Virginia reserved 6,570 square miles to satisfy the bounties promised to her Revolutionary soldiers. Large tracts of land were thus thrown on the market, and one of the nation's early land booms began.

Earliest of white settlements was that at the little village of Schoenbrunn on the Tuscarawas River. Here the Moravian missionaries, David Zeisberger and John Heckewelder, established themselves and their converts, and here were erected in 1772 the first schoolhouse and the first church in the confines of what is now the State of Ohio.

Following the disgraceful massacre of Christian Indians at Gnadenhutten in 1782, the Moravian settlements in the vicinity were abandoned and the site of Schoenbrunn forgotten. In recent years, however, it has been located, and the Ohio State Archaeological and Historical Society has built replicas of the log houses on the original sites.

The first permanent settlement was made on the Ohio River at the mouth of the Muskingum where in 1788 the city of Marietta was established. Here is still to be seen the little office of the Ohio Land Company (Plate 1), built within the stockade when the

PLATE 6: *Red Brick Tavern, Lafayette. Built in 1837*

[8]

town was founded, and known as the oldest building in the state. It is preserved as an historic monument.

Soon a tide of emigration set toward the West, flowing largely through two main channels. The first was over the Alleghenies from Virginia, Maryland, Pennsylvania, and the more southerly states, following the old trail along which Braddock and Washington traveled on their ill-fated expedition to Fort Duquesne. Coming to the present site of Pittsburgh, boats were built by the immigrants who floated down the Ohio River to their destinations. Later the Cumberland Pike, or National Road, was extended through Wheeling and across central Ohio to the west.

The more northerly route was across New York State to Buffalo, where some took ship on Lake Erie, while others followed its southern shore along the beach, or the old Indian trail, which eventually became the Buffalo-Detroit Road and now passes through Cleveland as Euclid Avenue.

This tide of immigration flowed to the west in such increasing volume that it threatened to depopulate the older states of the east, for the area now embraced in Ohio, which ranked in 1800 as eighteenth in population among the states, rose to fifth place in 1820, a gain that was made very largely at the expense of the eastern seaboard states. This menace to the east became so acute that efforts were made to curtail it; propaganda was employed and stories circulated to the effect that the western country was inhospitable, unhealthful, the soil infertile, and the forests filled with wild animals and wilder men. Even the cartoon was brought into play, and one that is still in existence shows a well-dressed man riding a well-groomed horse, both looking hopeful and happy. Beneath this is the inscription, "We are going to Ohio." The companion picture shows the same man, ragged, forlorn, and discouraged, the horse a poor old crow-bait, hungry and woebegone, apparently about to tumble into the ditch; and beneath this is the legend, "We have been to Ohio." In spite of all, the tide of immigration flowed on.

PLATE 7: *Penn Tavern, Middlebourne*

PLATE 8: *St. Charles Hotel, formerly The Mansion House, Marietta. Built in 1835*

[11]

PLATE 9: *Rider Tavern, Painesville. Probably built about 1822. Enlarged and portico added a few years later. Restored in 1922*

EARLY INNS

With humanity in such numbers plodding on foot or riding horseback and in slow-going vehicles, over poorly made roads, one of the vital necessities was adequate provision for the rest and refreshment at night of man and beast. Inns were built at frequent intervals, and today if you follow the Old National Road over the mountains of Maryland and Pennsylvania and across the more level stretches of Ohio, or that other route across New York State and along the lake, you will find many of the old inns of pioneer days. Other routes through Pennsylvania might be noted here, but these are the most famous.

One of the most interesting of the old stopping places is the Headley Inn (Plate 2) on the National Road four miles west of Zanesville. Built originally in 1802, it was enlarged in 1833 by the two-story addition on the east. It is substantially constructed of dressed stone, and the interior today is much as it was known in the past to the throngs of weary pioneers who stopped there on their way into the west. The large stone house, known as the Smith place, which stands a few yards away, was built in 1830. It is still occupied by descendants of the original builder who bought the inn from the Headley family.

The old fireplaces still remain in the inn; a crude little stairway (Plate 3) winds from the kitchen up beside the chimney to the attic above the second floor. In the kitchen is the great fireplace where the cooking was done for generations of travelers, and you still see where the stone jambs on either side of the fire opening have had the corners deeply worn away by the whetting of carving knives; mute witness perhaps to the quantity of tough beefsteak that was served to hungry boarders. Another interesting stairway (Plate 4) has a quaint and unusual decoration on the risers, in the form of flowing vines with leaves and flowers painted in colors. This same decoration is continued around the baseboard of two upstairs rooms.

PLATE 10: *Buckingham House, Zanesville. Built about 1834*

The Headley Inn was a popular stopping place on the National Road and witnessed many stirring events in its day, but with the coming of the railroads, traffic along the old highways ceased. The little towns that had been so prosperous went to sleep; the inns were closed, converted into dwellings, or perhaps destroyed.

Years have passed, and with the coming of the automobile, travelers again roll by, but softly and swiftly in rubber-shod motor cars instead of in creaking ox-drawn carts. Many of the old hostelries have come to life again, serving as tea rooms, or as hotels for auto tourists. Unlike many of these the Headley Inn has been most intelligently restored, as few changes as possible having been made, and the decoration on the old stairway, instead of being repainted, has been carefully washed and covered with a coat of varnish to insure its preservation.

Another famous stopping place on the National Road is the Red Brick Tavern (Plate 6) at Lafayette, between Columbus and Springfield. This fine old structure was built in 1837, as an investment by Stanley Watson from Connecticut, on land owned by his father-in-law, William Minter, a Revolutionary officer to whom had been granted 6,000 acres for military services. Recognizing the strategic value of this location, between two important towns, Minter laid out a town on his tract. He left the naming of it to his daughter, and she, having just read a biography of Lafayette, who was much in the public mind because of his recent visit to the country, named it after the French count.

Being one of the important places of entertainment on the famous road, the Red Brick Tavern was patronized by many distinguished persons of stagecoach days, among them being Martin Van Buren, William Henry Harrison, and Henry Clay.

The tavern had but one landlord, John McMullen, who managed it from 1837 to 1859. After that time tavern keeping on the stagecoach roads became unprofitable due to the advent of railroads, and the Red Brick Tavern, like many others, closed for lack of

PLATE 11: *Matthews House, Zanesville. This beautiful adaptation of the Greek Doric order suggests that the builder worked from plates such as were published by Asher Benjamin*

patronage. With the coming of the automobile it has been opened again to the public.

The story is told that when Mr. Van Buren was running for the presidency, he stopped at this tavern. A formal dinner was tendered him, and a Mrs. Minter, daughter-in-law of the town's founder, chose this affair to make first use of a fine new set of gold-band china, which she had recently acquired, but which she had refused to use until it could be initiated by some distinguished guest. Pieces of this set were exhibited recently at the tavern.

Henry Clay was accorded a more vital honor while a guest here. A baby born not far from Lafayette was promptly named after him and in recognition of the act Mr. Clay called at the home and presented the mother with five dollars as the nucleus of a bank account for the most recent acquirer of the name of Henry Clay.

Between Zanesville and Wheeling, in the little town of Middlebourne, is the old Penn Tavern (Plate 7), whose doorway is an interesting example of the architecture common at that time. The deeply-worn stone sill recalls the countless footsteps that have passed in and out, and some sort of moral might be aimed at the habits of our forebears because of the fact that the stone sill of the adjoining doorway, which led into the barroom, is even more deeply worn.

The old St. Charles Hotel, originally known as the Mansion House (Plate 8), at Marietta, has a fine entrance with a semi-circular fan light above, and a door which hinges in the middle, folding back like a shutter against the wall.

The Rider Tavern at Painesville (Plate 9), to which reference has been made, is distinguished by the imposing portico across the front, quite in keeping with that at Mount Vernon. These great square piers are built around rough-hewn timbers which form the actual support for the roof. A little door cut in the side of one of the piers enables the curious to examine this unusual construction.

This inn, which was on the verge of destruction a few years ago,

PLATE 12: *Guthrie House, Zanesville. Built in 1842-43 by George Nelson Guthrie who came from Concord, New Hampshire, in 1839. It is believed that Mr. Guthrie designed the house, at his wife's request, after a former home in Concord*

has been carefully restored, refurnished with antique furniture, a large dining room added at one end, and is once more in active service. Similar restoration was effected at the other Mount Vernon type tavern at Unionville.

ZANESVILLE

Four doorways, in that part of Zanesville formerly known as Putnam, give striking evidence of the versatility of the early Ohio builders. The old Buckingham House (Plate 10) has a doorway of unusual type, recessed within an arched opening, and crowned with a shell effect said to be made of sheet zinc. The doorway is in perfect condition today, excepting for the side lights, which were destroyed during the flood of 1913. A few blocks away is the Matthews House (Plate 11), a sturdy stone structure with a portico that reproduces, as perfectly as might be expected of even a master builder, the details of the Greek Doric temple.

The question is often asked, "How was it possible for the pioneer carpenters in a newly-settled country to produce such beautiful examples of classic architecture?" The answer is that their apprenticeship had been spent working on buildings of just such design and detail, and that they, fortunately, knew nothing else. Moreover, they doubtless brought with them from the east plates or books of designs showing such architectural forms and details. These books were much used, a series having been published by Asher Benjamin, a builder of Greenfield and Boston, Massachusetts, whose works found wide sale throughout the country, as did those of Minard Lafever. Both of these authors published plates, showing the Doric order, from which the Zanesville builder might well have studied the details of this portico (Plate 76).

A few steps down the street is the Guthrie House, of the classic temple type, whose stately portico is an impressive example of this style which was so common in the early nineteenth century. Distinction should be made between these Greek Revival houses, and those of the Colonial period. The former reproduce the general

PLATE 13: *Nye-Potts House, Zanesville. Built in 1813. The doorway, stone "stoop," iron hand rail, and brick sidewalk recall those of eastern Pennsylvania and Maryland*

effect of the classic temple, with its end to the street, the low-pitched roof projecting beyond the front wall, and supported by great columns, forming an imposing portico. (Plate 12.) The eighteenth century Colonial house, if not square, usually stands with its long face to the street. If there is a columned portico it is, with perhaps a few rare exceptions, a later addition (Plate 12).

Just around the corner from the Guthrie House stands the Nye-Potts House (Plate 13) originally built by Major Horace P. Nye. This is of the typical Philadelphia or Baltimore style, of red brick with stone trimmings, having a double-stone stoop and steps, with an iron hand rail leading down to the brick sidewalk. The door is surmounted by a semi-elliptical fan light, and on either side are colonnettes, but it is without the side lights which are so commonly found in the east after 1790. It is a curious fact that side lights were practically unknown before the Revolution, while they became quite the fashion a decade or two afterward. Whether this was due to a greater desire for privacy in Colonial days, or because curiosity to see passers-by developed as a byproduct of newly acquired freedom, is hard to tell. Gossip says that Philadelphia ladies circumvented the early handicap of side-lightless doors by attaching small mirrors to the casing of their front windows. Thus, while discreetly out of sight, they kept themselves, through the friendly service of the mirrors, adequately informed as to the habits, customs, and costumes of passing friends and rivals.

FIREPLACES

Within the Nye-Potts House are many interesting features, among them the window shutters made of four narrow boards hinged to fold into the pocket of the window casing. The simple mantel shown in the illustration is typical of the period and representative of the final stage in the evolution of the American fireplace (Plate 14).

The New England fireplace of the seventeenth century had a cavernous opening which consumed vast quantities of wood and

PLATE 14: *Nye-Potts House—Fireplace. The fire opening has been bricked up and a Franklin stove installed*

sent most of its heat up the great chimney. In time, as fuel became more costly, these were bricked in to smaller proportions until eventually fire openings were scaled down to about the size shown here, and even that extravagance was ultimately done away with by Benjamin Franklin's invention of the stove which bears his name. This open stove of cast iron stands in front of the fireplace, to which it is connected only by a small pipe of sufficient capacity to create a draft and carry off the smoke, thus providing a maximum of heat with a minimum of fuel. This invention became internationally known, and would have made Franklin famous had he done nothing else in his long lifetime.

About twenty miles up the Muskingum River from Zanesville, in the little town of Adams Mills, is the Adams-Gray House (Plate 15), in which two fireplaces (Plate 16) have facings that are extraordinary examples of cast-iron work. On either side of the opening are beautiful figures of Ceres bearing on their heads baskets of flowers and fruit; and above the opening a figure panel, also in low relief, illustrates the legend of Mazeppa. On it is shown a wild horse galloping at breakneck speed through the forest with the nude body of a man lashed to his back and a pack of wolves in pursuit.

Many cast-iron facings are to be found in old houses, but rarely showing such perfection of workmanship as these. The house was built by a Virginian, who may have had these facings shipped to him from one of the foundries in the east, such as Welford's in Philadelphia, or they may even have been imported from Europe. On the other hand it is quite possible that they were made in Ohio.

A STONE BRIDGE

The National Road has been mentioned a number of times, and it may not be amiss to digress for a moment from houses to the strange S bridges which are, or were, curious features of the road. These are of massive masonry, excellently designed and built, but with a curved plan that takes them across the streams in a meandering course that seems quite inexplicable.

PLATE 15: *Adams-Gray House, Adams Mills. Built in 1841 by Edward G. Adams. The Virginia origin of the builder is reflected in the wide central hall which serves as a well ventilated living room in summer*

On my first trip along the National Road, I stopped at several of these S bridges, among them the one just west of Hendrysburg (Plate 17), and after photographing it, discovered an inscription carved in the parapet which announced that this bridge was "Built in 1828 by John McCartney." A few rods east of the bridge stood an old brick building bearing the legend, "McCartney's Tavern." With curiosity whetted, I determined to ascertain the reason for all these crooked bridges. The question was propounded to a young woman sitting on the porch, who promptly replied, with a twinkle in her eye, that she guessed "the bridges were crooked because all the folks around there were crooked." She finally said, however, that the bridges in this part of the road were built by her husband's grandfather, John McCartney, and that according to a family tradition, after "Granddad McCartney," and the engineer in charge of construction had gotten well mellowed one Saturday evening in the barroom, the engineer made a rough plan of this bridge and tossing it across the table said, "McCartney, can you build that bridge?" The builder looked at the drawing for a moment and replied, "Sure, I can build any bridge you'll draw." The drawings were completed, the bridge erected, and the job was so well done that he was given a liberal bonus.

It really is an extraordinarily fine piece of masonry (Plate 18), massive enough to serve as the ramparts of a medieval castle or a section of the Chinese Wall; and all for the purpose of spanning a little creek across which I jumped with my tripod and camera.

This bridge was buried in 1933 in a fill of earth made necessary by road improvements. Every effort was made to save it, as has been done with other bridges along the road, but the expense involved was too great to warrant diverting the course of the highway.

HOUSES OF NEW ENGLAND TYPE VERSUS APARTMENTS

Returning again in our quest to the Western Reserve, we find the old houses to be largely of the sort that were built throughout

PLATE 16: *Adams-Gray House. The cast-iron facing is an unusual example of fine modeling and casting. Above the fire opening is a bas-relief showing the nude figure of a man, lashed to the back of a wild horse, and pursued by a pack of wolves, evidently illustrating the story of Mazeppa*

Connecticut and Massachusetts, simple frame buildings, the walls clapboarded, and often accented at the corners with flat pilasters, crudely adapted from the classic orders. The roofs are low in pitch, and the gable cornice mouldings return upon themselves.

In many instances a low L, running at right angles to the main block of the house, has a recessed porch, the lintel of which is supported by simple columns. The two shown from Ashtabula (Plate 19), and Mesopotamia (Plate 20), are of the same general type, but the owner of the latter was blessed apparently with more generous financial resources or a larger family, or both, and built accordingly.

I often think of the contrast between the living conditions of youngsters who have the good fortune to grow up in such surroundings, and the modern city child who lives in one of the up-to-date, four-room-in-one apartments. They are most comfortable and convenient for old folks, the unmarried, and newly-weds, but pity should go out to the children of these cliff-dwellers. With bedrooms consisting of the other side of closet doors, the luckless occupants must tuck themselves away where best they can on evenings when guests stay late.

Of course, these modern in-a-door and under-foot apartments are marvels of compactness and ingenuity, but they seem more akin to bee hives than to human dwellings.

I have a friend who lived, or existed, in an apartment that was just the last word. Its masterpiece was a bed in the bottom drawer of the sideboard. When inclined toward slumber, you stoop down, drag open the bottom drawer of the sideboard, crawl in and go to sleep.

The mother of my friend went a-calling one evening on a fellow cliff-dweller across the hall. Her knock brought no response for several minutes; then the door opened revealing the embarrassing fact that the gentleman of the house had retired in the bottom drawer of the sideboard. There was no other place to park him, so

PLATE 17: *S Bridge on National Road west of Hendrysburg. Built by John McCartney about 1828. Buried under a fill of earth during reconstruction of the road in 1933*

his resourceful wife merely closed the drawer until only his head was exposed, and then entertained her guest with perfect propriety.

Various Types of Houses

The old houses of Ohio are as a whole so simple that they seem to be monotonously alike, but it does not require long acquaintance to find that they are of infinite variety, especially the doorways. The old house on the road from Claridon to Burton (Plate 21), for instance, seems at first glance to be like a thousand others, and devoid of especial interest; yet examination of its doorway shows detail of unusual distinction, for carved on the frieze are oval medallions such as are common in work of the Brothers Adam, famous English architects of the late eighteenth century. Here in a remote rural community of northern Ohio is seen the influence that came from London, across the ocean to New England, and eventually found its way far out to the Western Reserve.

Close by on the same road is the old Hitchcock House (Plate 22), the doorway of which is quite reminiscent of those in Deerfield, Massachusetts. The hallway into which it opens is one of the few in Ohio which possesses that characteristic feature of the seventeenth century houses of New England—the steep, winding Jacobean staircase.

Going again to the southern part of the state, we will take the Scioto Trail from Columbus and, after passing through Circleville, will see on our left, perched on a gently sweeping knoll, Mount Oval, the old Renick-Young House (Plate 23) which was built in 1832. Here is seen distinctly the southern influence that was brought to the west over the National Road; but even in the south houses of this type are few and far between, the only one I recall being Mulberry Castle, at Goose Creek, South Carolina. (This unusual Jacobean house, which was built before 1725, has the semi-detached, one-story towers on each corner, but otherwise it has little resemblance to Mount Oval.)

The original owner of Mount Oval was William Renick, whose

PLATE 18: *Side view of S Bridge on National Road west of Hendrysburg*

parents came from Hardy County, Virginia. He became a successful breeder and dealer in cattle, a writer, and in many ways a "man
of parts." He was a nephew of Felix Renick who brought the first
thoroughbred Short Horn cattle from England to Ohio, and was
one of a group who introduced blue grass into Kentucky.

The central room of the house (Plate 24) is twenty-five feet
square and twelve feet high, and at each of three corners is a small
bedroom ten feet square and of equal height. The one at the right
(Plate 26), has no communication with other rooms, and was
reserved for the use of drovers who were frequently at the house on
business. Access to this room is gained from a recessed porch at
the side, similar to that in front. The porches are covered by the
main roof which sweeps upward from the corners and is accented
on the front by a rather over-large dormer window. At the left
the dining room and service quarters stretch back, occupying the
space that otherwise would have been occupied by another porch
and corner bedroom.

Entering the living room we find it to be of unusual size, with
trim of excellent design and fine workmanship. The mantel (Plate
25), the paneling of doors and jambs, and other details all testify
to the quality of this house. Fortunately its owners appreciate its
beauty, and maintain it in good condition. An interesting feature
of the recessed porches (Plate 148) is the ceiling, which has a
gentle arched curve from the eaves to the brick walls, and is made
up of longitudinal panels so narrow as to give the effect, at first
glance, of matched sheathing.

Another house that seems to show southern influence is the
Kinsman House (Plate 27) at Warren which, with its Ionic columns stretching the height of two stories, the very low entablature,
and the absence of a pediment has much more the effect of a southern plantation house than of a mansion in northern Ohio. This was
built in 1832 by Frederick Kinsman.

PLATE 19: *Typical New England farmhouse, near Ashtabula. The heavy pilasters and entablature, as well as the recessed porch, are common throughout the Western Reserve*

DOORWAYS

Now let us glance briefly at a number of doorways. The first (Plate 28), is of the type found so commonly throughout New England and the middle west, the door flanked by flat pilasters with Ionic or Doric caps supporting an overly heavy entablature. This doorway, with modifications as to proportions and details, may be found literally by the hundreds. The one in Athens (Plate 29) is a Colonial type that is unusual in Ohio, but quite common in the older portions of the east. The Guild doorway (Plate 30), in Eagleville is much simpler in design, but represents a great amount of labor in fitting the innumerable panels in the casing.

Here and there are unique designs that seem to reflect the individual taste of some local builder who crystallized his ideas or ideals on a few buildings entrusted to him, but when he passed from the picture none was sufficiently impressed to carry on the tradition. The doorway at Streetsboro (Plate 31) shows an evident attempt to reproduce a design of the Brothers Adam. The semi-elliptical overdoor was doubtless inspired by a print from some book of designs, and the builder, untrained in the field of architectural tradition, was unable to interpret the hints given in the small engraving. He did his best, and in place of the flutings and rosettes of Adam's work, he tacked on trios of half-round turnings, alternating them with what look like overfed stars. These prove on close examination to be circular adaptations of the elliptical sunbursts which are planted on the frieze, these in turn being crude attempts to interpret the details that have been so delicately executed on the Allen mantel (Plate 114). Variants of this doorway are to be found on the Treat House near Aurora, and on another in West Richfield.

Another type, found on the Mathews House at Painesville, has the curiously carved doorway placed between two-story pilasters. The door and the side lights are separated by reeded columns with Ionic capitals, and the transom is divided into three sections by

PLATE 20: *House at Mesopotamia*

[34]

corbels carved with acanthus leaves. Above these are square rosettes between which hang swags of carved drapery. Modifications of this unusual design are to be found on the Elwell House at Willoughby and the Warner House at Unionville. The front doorway of the Warner House, though similar to the others in design, seems to be a copy by a less able man than Goldsmith. The Mathews House, and probably the Elwell House as well, was designed and built by Jonathan Goldsmith, a man of unusual attainments who was responsible for much of the fine architecture in Lake County. (See page 95.) Nowhere else in the state have I seen doorways of this type.

A charming little doorway on which the door and side lights are flanked by dainty reeded colonnettes is found on the old Gates House (Plate 32) at Gates Mills, now remodeled and used by the Chagrin Valley Hunt Club. The overly heavy entablature is enriched by fine oval sunbursts similar to those on the Mastick-Moffett House near Burton (Plate 21). The Gates doorway has been carefully preserved, except for the door itself in which three panels have been replaced by glass. (The house burned in July, 1935, but devoted admirers managed to save the doorway which still graces the restored clubhouse.)

At Lancaster, once a city of much prominence in Ohio and the boyhood home of John and William Tecumseh Sherman, are a number of unusually fine houses. One of these, the Effinger House (Plate 33), was built by a Philadelphian in front of an old stage-coach tavern, which was retained for use as a service wing. The excellent doorway and the Palladian window above, with their stone casings, well-designed side lights, and elliptical fan lights are of unusual beauty. Within the hallway a spiral staircase (Plate 34) rose to the second floor, and the house contained mantels and other details of excellent design (Plate 174).

This house was destroyed a few years ago to make way for a motion-picture theatre, parking space, or some other of the modern

PLATE 21: *Mastick-Moffett House, near Burton*

[36]

PLATE 22: *Peter Hitchcock House, near Burton—Doorway. It is character-istically New England of the late eighteenth century, as might be expected, its builder having come from Connecticut. Built in 1807*

PLATE 23: *Renick-Young House (Mount Oval Farm), near Circleville. Built in 1832 by William Renick. The house is unique in plan, having a large central living room with bedrooms at three corners. The front bedroom at the right is entered only through a door from the side porch. This was for the use of cattlemen*

improvements that have sounded the death knell of so many good examples of architecture. Fortunately the doorway, window, part of the stairway, and other portions of the interior detail have been preserved by the Gallery of Fine Arts at Columbus.

The original plans and bill of materials are still in existence, the latter showing the cost of the stairway to have been two hundred dollars. The construction was excellent, stability being assured by iron rods running into the wall at every ninth step. This reinforcing was so well done that the house-wreckers found it impossible to take down the stairway until the wall was removed from around it.

AN OLD MILL

Although perhaps out of place in this discussion, I cannot resist introducing an illustration of the great overshot water wheel formerly at Wolfe's Mill (Plate 35) near Loudonville. It is difficult to realize that within the memory of living persons such wheels constituted practically the only source of power, excepting the horse, that was known or utilized in this country. This mill is particularly interesting because of the fact that all the water required for its operation flowed directly from springs through a flume, in sufficient volume to turn the wheel without the necessity for impounding it in a mill pond. The springs still yield the same abundance of pure water, but the machinery lies unused and almost intact within the mill. It is to be hoped that this mill may be preserved* as an historic monument to illustrate the vast strides that have been made in industrial development from this simple power house to the great plants of Cleveland, Youngstown, Warren, Lorain, and other industrial cities that have given to northern Ohio the name "Ruhr of America."

CHURCHES

Any discussion of New England people would be incomplete

---

*Since this was written, the machinery has been stripped from the mill in adapting it to use as a tea room. The great wheel has fallen to pieces and posterity has been robbed of just one more relic of the past.

PLATE 24: *Renick-Young House—Living room*

without reference to their religious life, and in northern Ohio we find (or could have found before progress swept so many of them away), that every town and village had its churches and steeples around which the houses clustered. Here again we can readily trace the origin of the early settlers, for these churches are very similar to those of New England.

The little church at Streetsboro (Plate 36) resembles those of many a New England town, and similar ones are to be found in Twinsburg, Brecksville, Gates Mill, and elsewhere in the Western Reserve. The majority of these were, of course, Congregational, for the settlers were largely of that denomination.

The church at Tallmadge (Plate 37) is probably the finest of the early Ohio churches, and compares favorably with all but the very best examples in New England. It was erected under the supervision of Colonel Lemuel Porter, who came from Waterbury, Connecticut, choosing Tallmadge as his western home because of its religious atmosphere. The great columns in front are reeded, not fluted, and it is said that they were made from solid walnut logs. The doors are still fitted with the original hinges, locks, and handles. The interior retains the flat dome and the balconies with their original pews, but in other ways it has lost much of its former beauty. At some time during the dark ages of the nineteenth century the fine, small-paned sash were replaced by "art glass" windows of sickly hue that were so popular at that time. On the occasion of the church's one hundredth anniversary, in 1925, these perversions of pseudo-glasiers were replaced by suitable sash with clear glass, and the shutters of the large front window were opened, disclosing beautifully patterned sash.

Another of Ohio's choicest architectural records of its early past is the church at Atwater (Plate 115). Little data regarding its construction or its designers and builders is available. Physical evidence, however, indicates that the steeple was added at a date later than that of the building's completion, 1841, for portions of the

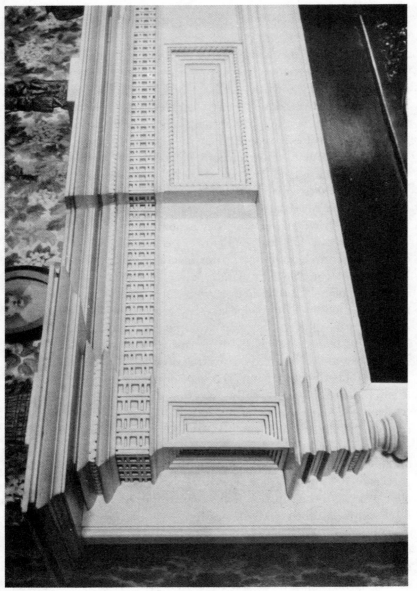

PLATE 25: *Renick-Young House—Detail of living room mantel*

original shingle roof still remain inside the tower. Then too the building seems too short to have been planned for a feature of such commanding size. The appearance of the steeple has been changed considerably, as shown in the photograph, by the loss of urn-shaped ornaments that originally stood at the corners of the square base, and above the columns that carry the lantern.

The interior of the church has been disfigured for many years by metal covering on the walls and ceiling, which has effectually concealed the flat dome, and also by a partition that encloses the gallery and gives the room a "snubbed off" appearance.

For a time fears were felt for the safety of the steeple, but in 1933 funds were raised which made possible certain absolutely essential repairs that insured its preservation. A set of chimes was installed at the same time in memory of a family of pioneer communicants.

The pointed windows are curiously at variance with the pure classicism of the portico and steeple, but this is a vagary commonly found in churches erected so near the border line between the Greek and Gothic Revivals.

Despite criticisms the Atwater church may well be regarded as in a class with the one at Tallmadge, and one of the finest of Ohio's early places of worship.

Another ecclesiastical structure, of less beauty but of outstanding historical importance, is the old Mormon Temple (Plate 41) at Kirtland, erected under the direction of Joseph Smith and Brigham Young, in the years 1833-1836. The story of its building is as dramatic, in a way, as that of King Solomon's Temple at Jerusalem. It is replete with legends of the sacrifices of the men who quarried and hauled the stone, and laid up the walls; of the women who raised the sheep, prepared the wool, and made the garments of those who labored on the temple; of the priests to whom angels revealed specifications for the building, and who prayed on the walls at night after the workmen had done with their day's labor.

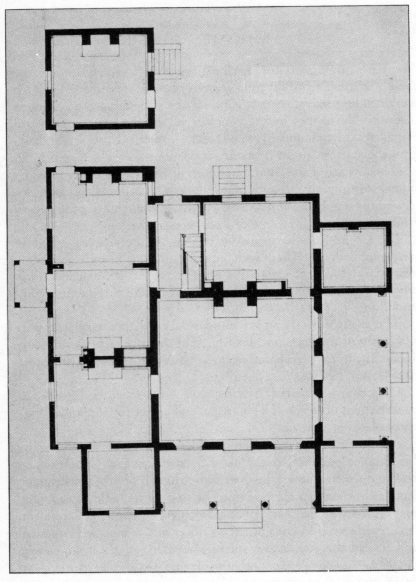

PLATE 26: *Renick-Young House—Floor plan. Living room in center, with towers at three corners. A most unusual arrangement. Reproduced by courtesy of Charles St. J. Chubb, Ohio State University.*

[44]

The story of Mormonism in Ohio is one of the most dramatic chapters in the state's history.

The interior of the building possesses much more of interest and beauty than does the exterior; indeed it is quite unique with its two auditoriums, one above the other, the grouped pulpits (Plate 42) at each end of the auditoriums, and the device for raising and lowering curtains by means of which the auditorium was divided into a series of small rooms during certain parts of the religious service. Further discussion of the Temple will be found on page 188.

THREE DISTINCTIVE HOUSES

A rare example of early Ohio architecture is to be found in the old Sinton Mansion (Plate 44), now the Taft Museum. It is somewhat similar in appearance to Homewood at Baltimore, and is unusually good in proportion and detail, being worthy of its present use as an art museum, bequeathed to the city of Cincinnati by the Honorable and Mrs. Charles P. Taft, whose home it was up to the time of their deaths.

The Avery-Downer House (Plate 45) at Granville is another fine example of Greek Revival design. It was built about 1842 for Alfred Avery by Benjamin Morgan, who is credited also with St. Luke's Episcopal Church at Granville, and with having been associated with the design of the State House at Columbus (Plate 127).

A little cottage (Plate 46) of distinction and charm stood near Painesville, on the main road from Cleveland to Buffalo. This was the home of Jonathan Goldsmith, whose work will be spoken of more fully in Part II. It was of a type common throughout western New York State, having a central block one story and a half in height, with one-story wings on each side, and windows in the upper story protected and concealed by cast iron or wooden grille work. In this case the grilles were of wood. The front was enriched by four simple pilasters in low relief. The low wings with their recessed porches gave to the house an appearance of restfulness and dignity. This cottage was destroyed by fire in 1927.

PLATE 27: *Residence of Judge Frederick Kinsman, Warren. Built in 1835 by Isaac Ladd who also built the Quimby House, the courthouse, and other structures of importance here*

EARLY HOMES OF OHIO

THE CLASSIC REVIVAL

Ohio, together with the rest of the country in the middle west, was built up in its early days largely with houses of the Classic Revival type. This movement was due to the initiative of Thomas Jefferson, whose admiration for Roman architecture and devotion to the formulas of Palladio (Italian architect of the sixteenth century), led him to design his home at Monticello, the Capitol at Richmond, and the buildings of the University of Virginia, all in the Roman style. He also had a hand in determining the type of public buildings that should be built in the new capital city on the Potomac, and was responsible for many other buildings, public and private. The success of Mr. Jefferson's architecture established a cult, and although the Roman Revival became, in the hands of his successors, a Greek Revival, classic buildings with their towering columned porticos, whether Roman or Greek, became the architectural fashion; and houses, churches, courthouses, and other public buildings of this type were sprinkled over the country as though the heavens had let loose a snow storm of white classic temples with white columns.

One of Mr. Jefferson's fads, if we may frivolously call it such, was the octagonal house, the suggestion for which was probably found by him in Volume II of Kent's *Designs of Inigo Jones*. This octagonal design appealed to Mr. Jefferson's natural love of geometry, and he drew up plans for such a house to be built at Pantops, a plantation near Monticello which he had given to his daughter, Maria, who married John W. Eppes. As she died before the house was begun he undertook its erection at Poplar Forest, an estate owned by him in Bedford County. The house at Poplar Forest has a large central room which originally rose to the skylight. Around this are four rectangular rooms with octagonal ends. The one in front is divided by a hallway which leads from the entrance to the central room, leaving a small bedroom on each side.

This type of house also made a popular appeal and octagonal

PLATE 28: *Doorway at Bath*

[48]

PLATE 29: *Doorway at Athens. Such doorways, common in the eastern states during the late eighteenth century, are not found often in Ohio*

PLATE 30: *Guild House, Eagleville*

houses are found, although in small numbers compared with the temple form, scattered throughout the country. A book devoted to the advantages, esthetic and practical, of octagonal houses was published in 1854 by one, O. S. Fowler, "Author of Various Works on Phrenology." Which of Mr. Fowler's diverse lines of scientific research has been more beneficial to human progress is problematical.

An octagonal house near Painesville (Plate 47) has a plan somewhat different and less symmetrical than that of Poplar Forest, and with a wing added at the southeast corner that gives material increase in roominess. This house is also unlike Poplar Forest in being definitely two stories in height, and in having a central chimney around which the stairway rises to the second floor. Back stairs are tucked away in a triangular space between the dining room and kitchen.

The four drawings (Plates 140, 141, 142, 143), which were made by students of the Cleveland School of Architecture, show the unusual plan, and the framing of roof and second-story ceiling.

The Classic Revival spread throughout the country, and today we find these temple forms, with their low-pitched pediments and supporting columns, everywhere from New Orleans to Quebec. Two curiously diverse houses of this type were built at Chagrin Falls. One (Plate 48), low seated and with scarcely an indication of foundations to raise it above the ground, seems admirably adapted to crown the raised ground on which it stands. The other (Plate 49), stands on a high basement in a manner quite adapted to its site in a valley. If these two houses could swap sites, both would appear quite absurd; the one on the hill top would look as though perched on stilts, the other as if half submerged in the mud of its valley. These early builders may have lacked in scholarly training, but they certainly made up for it in common sense.

At Norwalk, early metropolis of the Firelands, are a number of fine classic houses. The Sturgis-Kennan House is distinguished by

PLATE 31: *Doorway of Singletary House, Streetsboro*

a portico with octagonal columns supporting the pediment, on which is a large oval sunburst (Plate 190). Further comment on the architecture of this town will be found in Part VIII.

HUDSON

The village of Hudson possesses a number of interesting houses and college buildings, as here was established, in 1826, Western Reserve College, the forerunner of Western Reserve University. It was often referred to as the "Yale of the West," as its original faculty was composed entirely of Yale men. From this college graduated a surprising number of men whose careers have taken them into positions of trust and prominence in the political, educational, and business worlds. Here was established the third astronomical observatory in the United States, in which Professor Elias Loomis made observations and wrote books that have given him a place among the great mathematicians and astronomers of the country. Here he devised the weather maps that are used today by the government weather bureau.

The little gambrel-roofed cottage known as the Hosford House (Plate 50) is one of the few examples of this type of house in northern Ohio. Common enough in Connecticut, the form was rarely reproduced here. This is probably due to the change in architectural fashions, for with Ohio pioneers becoming firmly established and economically independent about the time that Mr. Jefferson's Classic Revival was sweeping the country, and with Colonial styles regarded as old fashioned, our up-to-date ancestors built mostly in the manner popular at the time.

Oldest of Hudson houses, and reputed to be the oldest in the Western Reserve, is the Hudson-Lee House (Plate 51), that was built in 1806 by David Hudson, founder of the village. The house was sadly remodeled during the dour seventies, but in late years it has been restored to much of its former appearance on the exterior. The doorway is apparently original, except for the door itself which is of a later vintage. Chimneys, fireplaces, and partitions were

PLATE 32: *Doorway of Gates House (now the Chagrin Valley Hunt Club), Gates Mills*

[54]

removed when the house was remodeled, leaving but little of the interior to recall its appearance a century ago.

David Hudson, original settler of the village, left his home at Goshen, Connecticut, in 1799 to investigate the "swamp township" which he and five associates had purchased for fifty-two cents per acre. Ten thousand acres, in another township, were thrown in for good measure because of the undesirability of the original tract, thus reducing the purchase price to about thirty-four cents, certainly a reasonable figure in view of present values.

The Hudson family, which included his wife and six children, started for the west on January 1, 1800, accompanied by a party numbering thirty in all. They reached the mouth of the Cuyahoga River on May 28th, and from the village which Moses Cleaveland had settled there they started for Hudson, where they arrived at about the same time as the herd of cattle which one of the party had driven from western New York state.

The builder of this old house came honestly enough by the love of adventure which lured him to the west, for he was a lineal descendant, six generations removed, of Henry Hudson who sailed his *Half Moon* up the Hudson River.

A substantial brick house of Hudson was the home of Professor Nathan P. Seymour, professor of Greek at the old college and father of the more famous Professor Thomas D. Seymour of Yale. It is quite obvious that a man of his attainments would have the portal (Plate 52) of his house designed as nearly as possible in conformity with the ideals of the Greeks, whose culture was his life study.

Old North College has but little aside from its doorway to claim architectural distinction, but around it clusters much of college history. It was one of the first buildings erected and was designed as a dormitory for theological students. Not far from it is the old dining hall of the college where hordes of hungry boys came three times a day for the simple meals that were served. Most fascinating

PLATE 33: *Effinger House, Lancaster. Built in 1823; torn down in 1929*

[56]

memories of these old buildings were recalled in an article entitled "Hardscrabble Hellas," written by Lucien Price, published in the *Atlantic Monthly* of February, 1927, and later reprinted as a Christmas greeting by Western Reserve Academy.

This dining hall was managed for many years by a Mrs. Slaughter, and was accordingly dubbed "The Slaughter House." Here the hungry rabble pounded the tables and intoned their uncomplimentary dirge, which ran:

> Baked potato, mashed potato,
> Hash, mince pie;
> Stewed prunes, and cabbage soup—
> Oh! . . . . . My!

The doorway (Plate 53) is one of the most interesting in the town. It is evidently the crude interpretation, by an untrained carpenter, of an Adam design. Again, as on the Streetsboro doorway, he was unfamiliar with flutings and rosettes, and for them substituted half-round turnings and what look amazingly like wooden doughnuts appliquéd on the architrave. The effect, however, was fairly good, though not as successful as the radiating lines of sunburst over the door, a detail with which he was doubtless more familiar, as it was commonly used on the fan lights of gables. Examples of such fan lights (Plates 151-160) are to be found on this house and on many others in the vicinity.

The chapel (Plate 54), completed in 1836, was, of course, the center of college life and moreover has much of architectural interest to commend it. The detail of the entablature is well studied and the side walls are relieved by a series of blind arches which carry up to the entablature. The front is given a more academic treatment by the introduction of classic pilasters.

The old college records are as little concerned with the identity of the persons actually responsible for designing the building as were most records of the time. Designing, brick-laying, and carpentering were all in the day's work, evidently, and no laurel

PLATE 34: *Effinger House—Stairway*

[58]

wreaths were bestowed upon the man whose mind conceived the design. Some light is thrown on the subject, however, by resolutions adopted at a meeting of the trustees on August 26, 1834. These read:

"Resolved, that as soon as adequate funds can be obtained the Trustees will proceed to erect another college building for a Chapel, Cabinet, Library rooms, etc.

"Resolved that Messrs. Pierce, Pitkin, and Bradstreet be a committee to draw a plan for the contemplated Chapel."

The three men named on this committee were, without doubt, George Edmond Pierce, president of the college from 1834 to 1855; Rev. Caleb Pitkin, and Stephen I. Bradstreet, trustees. A year later Caleb Pitkin was entrusted with the doubtful privilege of collecting funds, superintending the building of the chapel, meeting payrolls, and paying for materials. His efficiency in this usually thankless task is evidenced by another entry in the Trustees' records, dated August 23, 1836, which states that "During the recess the College Chapel was dedicated to the service of Almighty God agreeably to the previous resolution of the Board."

Whether the distinguished committee of three evolved the design for the chapel, or merely determined its general plan and left elevations and details to the discretion of men on the job, no one seems to know. The latter method was customary, and we may infer that the result is to be credited to the committee plus competent master builders.

What tales this old chapel might tell of distinguished speakers within; of the tongue which disappeared from the old bell, and was said to have been built into the masonry of a house that was under construction; of the live calf which was misplaced in the belfry!

North of the campus stands the cottage (Plate 55) formerly occupied by Professor Edward W. Morley. Professor Morley with Professor Michelson conducted the experiments in ether drift upon which was built the Einstein Theory. Here Professor Morley lived

PLATE 35: *Wolfe's Mill, near Loudonville*

while teaching in the college, his laboratory being in the old Athenæum, a few hundred feet behind the house, and here he conducted the experiments which brought to him recognition as one of the leading chemists of America. In later life he became president of the American Chemical Society. It is said that he rigged up a telegraph line from the laboratory to his house, and that at eleven o'clock he was wont to call his wife and tick off a message something like this, "It is eleven o'clock, my dear, I think you had better put the potatoes on to boil."

One of the finest houses of Hudson is the Baldwin-Buss House (Plate 56), with a façade distinguished by flat pilasters with Ionic capitals, and an arched doorway that gives it unusual style. Its formal dignity is relieved somewhat by the low wing extending to the left. This fine façade has been butchered in recent years by an ugly porch built across the front, cutting brutally into the pilasters and effectually concealing the doorway. It has not caused irreparable damage, however, and it is to be hoped that some day it will be removed and the house restored to its original appearance.

Another architectural tragedy is seen in the old Quinby House (Plate 57) at Warren, the stately Ionic portico being about all that recalls the glory of this once splendid mansion. (Since this was written, the house has been torn down.)

Thus, one by one, these old structures disappear. Their loss is not merely the destruction of wood, stone, and brick work; it is more, for these houses and churches are human documents that tell the story of those who built them, and lived or worshiped in them. We build monuments to the memory of heroes. These structures are monuments erected by the heroes themselves. Through them we may read, if we possess the discerning eye and mind, something of the character of the pioneers who came here to the wilderness, known as the Ohio Country, and laid foundations for the culture that places Ohio today among the foremost states of the Union.

PLATE 36: *Congregational Church, Streetsboro. Built in 1851*

PLATE 37: *Congregational Church, Tallmadge*

[63]

PLATE 38: *Congregational Church—Portico*

PLATE 39: *Congregational Church—Belfry*

[65]

PLATE 40: *Congregational Church—Detail of front*

PLATE 41: *Mormon Temple, Kirtland. Built in 1833-36*

[67]

PLATE 42: *Mormon Temple—Pulpits*

[68]

PLATE 43: *Mormon Temple—Detail of Pulpits*

[69]

PLATE 44: *Sinton-Taft House, Cincinnati. (Now the Taft Museum)*

PLATE 44A: *Sinton-Taft House—Doorway (Now the Taft Museum)*

[71]

PLATE 45: *Avery-Downer House, Granville. Built about 1842*

PLATE 46: *Jonathan Goldsmith Cottage, Painesville. Built in 1841. De-stroyed by fire in 1927*

[73]

PLATE 47: *Octagon House, Painesville*

[74]

PLATE 48: *Chagrin Falls, Cuyahoga County*

[75]

PLATE 49: *Bentley-Kent House, Chagrin Falls*

PLATE 50: *Hosford House, Hudson. Built in 1832*

PLATE 51: *Hudson-Lee House, Hudson—Doorway. Built in 1806*

[78]

PLATE 52: *Seymour House, Hudson*

[79]

PLATE 53: *Western Reserve College, Hudson—Doorway of old dining hall. The design reflects Adam influence, but interpreted with the crude originality of a carpenter untrained in architectural detail*

[80]

PLATE 54: *Western Reserve College—The Chapel*

[81]

PLATE 55: *Morley House, Hudson*

[82]

PLATE 56: *Baldwin-Buss House, Hudson. Built in 1825*

PLATE 57: *Quinby House, Warren. Designed and built by Isaac Ladd. Torn down in 1931*

PART II

THE EARLY BUILDERS

PLATE 58: *Bank of Geauga (later called Painesville National Bank). Painesville. Designed and built by Jonathan Goldsmith. Destroyed by fire in 1925*

[86]

PART II: THE EARLY BUILDERS

THE tragic destruction and mutilation of old buildings throughout our state, in the name of progress and improvement, is gradually but surely erasing the picture of pioneer Ohio and replacing it with one that reflects little of our early culture. Excepting as patriotic organizations, occasional lovers of fine architecture, and societies for the preservation of local antiquities check natural decay, and halt the hand of the "improver" and wrecker, few of our architectural landmarks will long survive. Unlike Europe, we give scant heed to our antiquities, and care little that they afford us almost our only visual evidence of past pioneer days.

Less permanent even than the structures themselves are the memories of their builders. The men whose minds conceived the designs for these early buildings and whose skillful hands transmuted the designs into structures of timber, brick and stone, have received scant recognition of their ability. To the historian they were mere workmen; the pages of history were sacred to the memory of politicians, lawyers, ministers, soldiers, and physicians. Only those who fought with ballot boxes, writs, devils, armies, and disease were worthy of preservation in the pages of history, and so the men were ignored who made the villages and countryside beautiful with homes for the great ones and places of worship for the Deity.

Today it is most difficult to write authoritatively of those master builders, or even to list their names. Here and there records are found of carpenters, masons, and builders, but little distinction is made between the workman who merely laid brick or hammered nails, and the highly trained master craftsman who could with equal facility draw an order, make a plan, carve an acanthus leaf or lay out a winding stair rail.

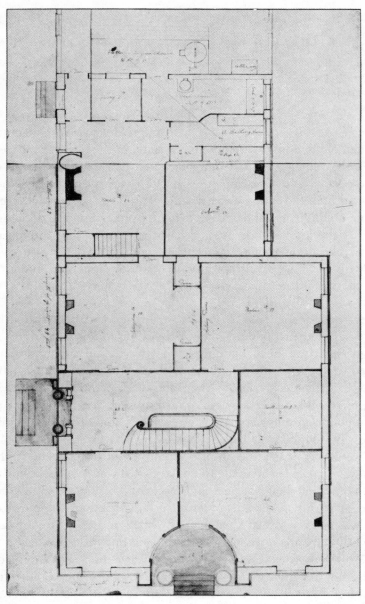

PLATE 59: *Original drawing for Bank of Geauga by Jonathan Goldsmith*

[88]

Here and there throughout the state it is possible to locate groups of buildings so superior in design and execution as to afford unmistakable evidence that here dwelt a man of ability, if not of genius, whose knowledge of building construction, and of at least the fundamentals of architecture, entitled him to a place of honor in the architectural profession.

Most of these men received their training as apprentices in the east or occasionally in England. Their skill with tools, including the pencil, was augmented by learning derived from prized though scanty libraries, in which were found books such as those of Asher Benjamin, Edward Shaw, and Minard Lafever, with perhaps an occasional volume by Batty Langley, or some other English writer of books for the house builder.

Today the names of these master craftsmen are unearthed only by the most patient searching. Rarely are their books or their drawings to be found. If preserved, these books and drawings are presumably stored away in attics, and old chests, perhaps forgotten even by the present owners, and almost impossible of discovery by the searcher for such documents.

In undertaking this particular study a start was made with lists of builders, carpenters, and masons, but it soon became evident that the assembling of such a roster was not only hopeless but useless. The records found were so vague as to afford little possibility for discriminating between laborers and highly trained craftsmen, hence it seemed best to restrict the search to a few master builders regarding whom reliable and reasonably complete records had been preserved, and let these suggest the stories of the many unknown but perhaps equally capable contemporaries.

As time goes on it is to be hoped that really comprehensive records will be made, but whoever attempts the search for this information will find himself confronted by no easy task, as has been proven by the great difficulties experienced in securing the meager data on which these few accounts are based.

Mere chance often plays an important part in such a search. For instance, a newspaper clipping in the hands of a friend led to the discovery of Jonathan Goldsmith's drawings; the Joseph Barker records were secured through the interest of a university professor, one of whose graduate students was engaged in research work for a thesis devoted to the early builders of Marietta. The drawing reproduced on Plate 69 is one of two discovered by a friend in an antique shop. They are practically identical and show a Greek Revival house with a story and a half central block from which low wings extend on either side. Black ink was used on white paper; grey washes emphasize columns and mouldings; the foundation is in a reddish brown wash; shutters are green, and curtains pink. On one drawing is the memorandum "51 feet front" and the signature "John C. Smith." This is apparently a later copy of the other, which bears no writing but has the scale indicated below the elevation. Nothing is known regarding either drawing or draftsman.

COLONEL LEMUEL PORTER

Among the few early builders of Ohio, who may be rightfully regarded as architects, was Colonel Lemuel Porter. Born in Sandisfield, Berkshire County, Connecticut, on January 20, 1775, he was apprenticed to Captain Lemuel Harrison of Waterbury, Connecticut, at the age of fourteen, to learn the joiner's trade. He drifted in time into the employ of Harrison's brother James, a maker of wooden-wheeled clocks, where he was said to have been a fellow apprentice with David Hoadley who afterward became famous as the architect of numerous churches in the vicinity of New Haven and Waterbury.

Becoming enamored of a certain Miss Margaret Anah Welton, he revealed a devotion which was apparently received with greater favor by the daughter than by her paternal parent who was a manufacturer of guns, and may have considered the young maker of clock wheels hardly the social equal of his daughter. At any rate the story goes that he finally told young Porter to leave his home

PLATE 60: *Original drawing for Bank of Geauga by Jonathan Goldsmith*

PLATE 61: *Plan and elevation of house by Jonathan Goldsmith. Drawing is signed with his name, but has no title or notes to make possible its identification*

and never to return until he invited him. A half hour later a knock was heard on the Welton front door. In response to the call "come in" from the head of the house, in walked Lemuel Porter. Evidently the father had a sense of humor, for in due time the young couple married.

During the business stagnation which followed the War of 1812 Porter sustained losses which prompted him to seek a home in the west and finding the social, civil, and religious life at Tallmadge, Ohio, much to his liking, he brought his family there in 1818.

He built various houses in the neighborhood and in 1822 was employed to superintend the "joiner work" on the Congregational church which was being erected at Tallmadge. Sabbens Saxton was the boss carpenter. Monday, the 24th day of December, 1821, was chosen as the day on which the timber was to be drawn to the village green. It was all drawn on that one day, coming in from all the eight roads that radiate from the town. The first log reached the scene of action before one o'clock in the morning, and Amadeus N. Sperry, who thus won the prize offered for the achievement, swore that he did not break the Sabbath day in making the record.

The shingles were all made from one chestnut tree, and it was intended that all the siding should be cut from a huge whitewood donated by Deacon Sackett. The tree was so large, however, necessitating so much loss in cutting it down to the capacity of the saw mill that this plan was not realized. The four columns on the front of the church were made from solid walnut logs, shaped and reeded by hand.

The high pulpit stood originally at the end of the church, on a level with the gallery, and was entered from the vestibule by winding stairs. The pews were square, with doors at the aisles. Work was finished and the church dedicated in 1825.

In 1849 the church was remodeled with rather disastrous results, but in 1925 when the centennial of its dedication was celebrated, the small pane sash were restored to the windows and other needed repairs were made. (See page 41).

PLATE 62: *Perspective drawing of a business block by Jonathan Goldsmith. It is signed but bears no notes or memoranda*

In 1826 Colonel Porter was given the contract for the first building of Western Reserve College at Hudson, and in 1829 the trustees employed him to do the carpenter and "joiner" work on the chapel. This was probably the building known as South College, as the present chapel was not built until about 1836. He moved his family to Hudson in the spring of 1829, and died suddenly on September 5th following, at the age of fifty-five years. He was buried at Tallmadge.

SIMEON C. PORTER

Following the death of Colonel Porter, his son Simeon was appointed by the college trustees to fulfill the contract for building the chapel. He had worked with his father at the joiner's and carpenter's trades and had devoted much time to the study of architecture. Continuing with the same workmen his father had employed, the chapel was completed to the full satisfaction of the college authorities.

The successful outcome of this contract brought to the younger Porter all the work he could do, in and around Hudson, and he maintained an effective organization of mechanics, including apprentices and journeymen. He removed eventually to Cleveland where we find him in partnership with Charles W. Heard, the city directory of 1856 listing the firm as Heard and Porter, Architects. On page 107 is further mention of this firm.

JONATHAN GOLDSMITH

In and about Painesville, and in fact throughout Lake County and the country adjacent, are to be found numerous old buildings of unusual character, both in design and construction, a large number of which were the creations of Jonathan Goldsmith. He was a person of importance, in his day; a man of wealth and, judging from the work left by him, possessed of unusual artistic attainments. Today he is almost forgotten, and it has been a most difficult task to assemble the following information regarding the man and his accomplishments.

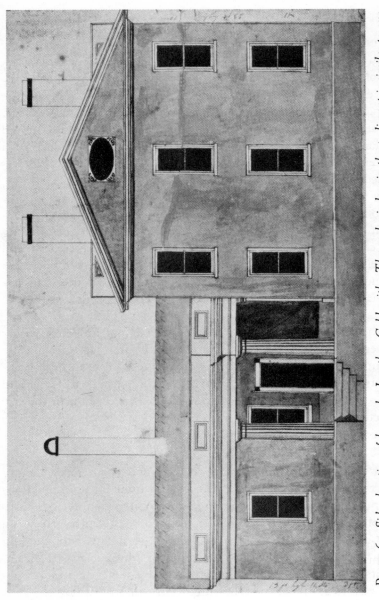

PLATE 63: *Side elevation of house by Jonathan Goldsmith. The oval window in the pediment is similar to one on the Morley House in Painesville. The drawing bears no signature or notes except figures giving dimensions*

Jonathan Goldsmith was born in September, 1783, at New Haven, Connecticut. His father was a vessel master, and died at sea of smallpox, leaving a widow and three children. Jonathan, aged eleven, was bound out to a shoemaker, but when seventeen he "bought" the balance of his time and apprenticed himself to a "carpenter and joiner" until twenty-one. Determined to master his trade he read everything available on architecture, and purchased architectural works as he could afford them. Though deprived of school advantages in childhood, he was an inveterate reader of good books throughout his life.

He removed to Hinsdale, Massachusetts, in 1804, where he bought land and built a house which Lucia Goldsmith, in her manuscript memoir of her father, says was "second to none for finish or convenience and free from debt." Here, in 1808, he brought his wife Abigail Jones (born 1786, died 1887, aged 101), together with her parents, three sisters, and two brothers.

It is said that he had made a previous trip to Painesville in 1802, but finding only a tiny settlement of log houses, with no need for services such as his, he returned to Massachusetts.

Finally in 1811 he came to "New Connecticut" with his wife and two children, travelling in a covered wagon with a yoke of oxen and a horse as leader. They endured all the perils and hardships of the pioneer immigrants, at one time nearly losing their lives when the oxen became frightened, on a high narrow bridge without railings, and dragged the wagon wheels within a tire's width of the edge.

With his two trades, shoemaking and housebuilding, Goldsmith contrived to make a living, and pay for help while clearing his farm. The War of 1812 brought fresh dangers. Goldsmith volunteered and went to "Maumee River," where he remained until sent back in charge of an open boat loaded with the sick. He himself became ill, reaching home with difficulty, and was confined to his bed for three months.

PLATE 64: *Dr. John H. Mathews House, Painesville. Built by Jonathan Goldsmith in 1829*

Rumors during the war of the depredations by British and Indians were responsible for alarms that on one occasion, when he was absent, caused Mrs. Goldsmith with two neighbor women and four children to hide for a night in their corn field.

The original log cabin was replaced by a frame house which Goldsmith commenced in the fall of 1818. The main block of this house was thirty-eight by twenty-six feet, with a wing on each side of twenty feet frontage, each having a gallery eight feet wide. The frame was twenty-five feet high from the brick foundation wall to the eaves. The cellar was six feet six inches below grade, with a stone wall, which was surmounted by two feet of brick wall above grade. His daughter writes of this, "The dining room was of oak and walnut, oiled and polished. The mantel, of walnut, was beautifully carved by himself. The glass, nails and trimmings came from Pittsburgh by teams." This house was burned.

In 1841 he built a cottage (Plate 46) a short distance west, which he occupied until his death in 1847. This passed eventually with the real estate into the hands of the Lake County Agricultural Society, and stood beside the fair buildings until destroyed by fire, April 27, 1927.

This cottage was a delightful little building, the two wings tying in most effectively with the low pitched hip roof, while pierced grills in the frieze provided a telling bit of enrichment that effectively accented the simple façade with its flat pilasters.

On his billheads Goldsmith designated himself as "Architect-Builder," and during the many years that he was engaged actively in building operations he made a most important contribution to the architecture of his vicinity. His clientele was not confined to his own town, for it is definitely known that he built houses in Mentor, Willoughby, Cleveland, and elsewhere.

One of the finest of his houses is that built for Dr. John H. Mathews (Plate 64) on North State Street, Painesville. This is one of three designed for various members of the Mathews family, the one built for Stephen Mathews now being used as a nurses' home by the local hospital. Three more were built for the three daughters of Isaac Gillett, two of which still stand.

The unusual design of Dr. Mathews' doorway was repeated with variations on the Elwell House of Willoughby, and the Warner House of Unionville, both of which definitely show the Goldsmith earmarks. Although these have not been authenticated as his work, there is every reason for attributing the Elwell House to him.

The old Painesville National Bank Building (Plate 58) that burned in 1925, was built by Goldsmith at the corner of Main Street and the Park. The drawings for this building are still in existence (Plates 59-60), as are the drawings, specifications, and bills of materials and labor for the original lighthouse and wharf which he designed for the mouth of Grand River. These drawings and those for residences (Plate 61) and other buildings show unusual skill as a draftsman; while his completed work proves that he was well-versed in architecture and in the details of building. (Plate 184).

He displayed a preference for the house plan with a central block flanked on either side by low wings, an idea derived presumably from books such as those of Asher Benjamin and Minard Lafever. Goldsmith developed this type of house surpassingly well in the Dr. Mathews House (Plate 64) and his own cottage (Plate 46). It is not so successful in the Elwell House at Willoughby, which we may presume to be his work. Here the wings are too small and sit back too far to form an effective composition. The Stephen Mathews House (Plate 66), has lost much of its original appearance, as the wings have been raised to a height of two stories and an ugly porch has been built across the front of the central block.

Another of his important Painesville houses was built for Albert Morley on North State Street. This is of brick and has an oval window (Plate 67) on the third story identical with one shown in the gable of the original drawing reproduced on Plate 63.

PLATE 65: *Dr. John H. Mathews House—Doorway*

PLATE 66: *Stephen Mathews House, Painesville. Completed in 1831.
Built by Jonathan Goldsmith*

Among other buildings in Painesville that are accredited to Goldsmith are St. James Episcopal Church; the original building of Lake Erie Female Seminary, now Lake Erie College, and the National Bank Building to which reference has been made. His granddaughter states that while drawing plans for the latter, he visited several eastern cities to study bank vaults, and as a result constructed one here that was pronounced "second to none in the country."

He built the Rider Tavern (Plate 9) and the Olds Stage House a short distance west, the latter for his brother-in-law, James Olds. So many dates have been assigned to the Rider Tavern that it is unsafe to be too positive regarding the matter. However, some confidence may be placed in an old letter that was found in Painesville, in which someone connected with the Goldsmith family purported to list buildings erected by Jonathan Goldsmith. Here the statement is made that Joseph Rider's first tavern was a one-story building that was erected in 1818 on the south side of Mentor Avenue. The existing building was built in 1822 and was raised and enlarged later, at which time the columns in front were added.

This old building is a distinguished adaptation of the Mount Vernon design with six square pillars, inside of which are solid hewn timbers that serve as the actual roof supports. The building was restored in 1922, once more becoming a tavern. The Olds Tavern was sold in the early thirties and since then has been in use as a private residence.

The old Mountain House (long since destroyed) and a smaller inn at Leroy (now quite ruinous) were also by Goldsmith, and all four are said to have had spring floors in their ballrooms, an innovation that he was first to introduce in the west.

Among the drawings by him, that still exist, is one showing a good-sized business block (Plate 62) and another that is evidently a design for a courthouse. The business block is well designed, and the drawing shows a very creditable knowledge of perspective; the

PLATE 67: *Morley House, Painesville—Gable Window. Built by Jonathan Goldsmith. This window is identical in design with that on original drawing by Goldsmith, Plate 63*

other leaves much to be desired. As a whole, however, the drawings are well executed and compare favorably with those of most American architectural draftsmen of the time.

Goldsmith made his drawings on various kinds of detail paper and used a brownish ink, at least it is brown now, washing in sections and walls with sepia and yellow. Elevations and perspectives were often made quite colorful, as for instance the one shown on Plate 61. Here the stone is in grey, the woodwork sepia, window sash red, muntins, doors, and transom ornament yellow, and the roof blue.

The first lighthouse at Fairport is shown on another of his existing drawings, together with bill of materials. Another bill covers timber for the wooden piers at the harbor. Still another drawing is a study for a "proposed reservoir and aqueduct at Fairport." He also built a railway from Painesville to Fairport, the rails being of wood and the motive power horses. While building the lighthouse he drove in a wagon to Erie to get the rope and tackle to be used in hoisting the lantern to the top of the tower. His daughter recalls that it was the longest rope she ever saw and filled the entire back of the wagon.

A number of important houses were built by Goldsmith in Cleveland, the finest being the Cowles House (1833) on Euclid Avenue, which was sold, after Mr. Cowles' death, and enlarged for the use of Ursaline Convent. This was a landmark on the avenue until torn down to make way for business.

Another Euclid Avenue house was built for S. J. Andrews, who was so pleased with the house that he presented the architect with a fine watch, to which Mrs. Andrews added a richly engraved gold key.

Work on the Andrews House was placed in charge of Goldsmith's son-in-law, Charles W. Heard, this being the young man's first job as "boss-journeyman." Heard had been an apprentice to Goldsmith, had lived in his home, and in 1830 married his elder

PLATE 68: *House near Medina. Built in 1854 by Burritt Blakeslee, and still occupied by his descendants*

daughter, Caroline Jones Goldsmith. He carried on his father-in-law's business in Cleveland and eventually became one of the city's leading architects and a man of means. He built and owned the Heard Block on the corner of Euclid Avenue and Sheriff (now East 4th) Street, of which part of the ground floor was used as a lobby for the Euclid Avenue Opera House.

Charles W. Heard formed a partnership with Simeon Porter (see page 95) thus bringing together two of the records that have been so carefully pieced together for this chapter; one beginning in Berkshire County, Massachusetts, with the birth of Lemuel Porter and coming to Cleveland by way of Tallmadge and Hudson; the other originating with Jonathan Goldsmith's birth at New Haven, Connecticut, and reaching Cleveland by way of Painesville.

Heard's name appeared in the city directory for more than twenty-five years. In 1837 he was listed as a carpenter; in 1856 he was associated with the firm of Heard and Porter, Architects; and in 1873 thirteen architects are listed, among them being Heard and Son.

BURRITT BLAKESLEE

The life and career of Burritt Blakeslee may be regarded as typical of the greater number of those master builders to whose skill we are indebted for the fine early architecture of our state. The following brief account of his life is taken from a letter written in 1926 by his granddaughter, Miss Mary Blakeslee:

"Burritt Blakeslee came to Ohio in 1816, at the age of 16 years, in an oxcart from Waterbury, Conn. The family settled here (at Medina) buying the land from Elisha Boardman, an officer in the Continental Army and member of the Continental Congress.

". . . . . . In a few years Burritt's father replaced the log house with the house which is still standing. . . . . . . a good example of our early architecture.

"On my grandfather's marriage, he built his home a quarter of a mile from the old place. He lost two houses by fire and built the third (Plate 68) on the same spot.

PLATE 69: Scale elevation in black ink and water color. The shutters are green, the foundation reddish brown, and the curtains ecru. A duplicate of this drawing is signed John C. Smith. (Reproduced by courtesy of Harry Hall White)

"As his sons grew up he devoted his time more especially to building and 'laid out' houses, as they used to say, He was a most careful and precise workman; his inside finishing was most exactly done, doors and woodwork being made by hand.

"Our house and one other, his brother's, are well finished examples of the period, showing the influence of Asher Benjamin.

"Graining was just coming in fashion when he built the third house. He was much interested, cutting samples of wood to get the natural grain, a rather useless effort.

"In the line of cabinet work he made all the caskets for the community. They were of black walnut and sold for six dollars apiece. He did smaller things in cabinet work, but I do not know of any furniture.

"My grandfather also had a sawmill and wool carding mill on Rocky River, run by a big water wheel.

"He belonged to the pioneer times when the shoemaker and the tailor came once a year to make the shoes and the clothes. He was a strong and self-reliant man who left a decided impression on his time. If he wanted a tool he could forge it.

"The old orchards of this vicinity show the interest he took in fruit growing and grafting. A book on fruit growing, and Benjamin's "Practical Carpenter" are the only books we have of his, other than an old account book. He died at the age of 66."

These notes give vivid impressions of the varied activities of the pioneer builder. What a commentary on the unionized specialization of today! Carpentry, cabinet work, graining, wool carding, coffin building, and blacksmithing were all in the day's work with men like Burritt Blakeslee.

These pioneer craftsmen were trained in the schools of hardship, privation, and hard work. Necessity begot versatility. If one house burned, they built another. With limited means and the simplest of tools and equipment they lavished the finest of workmanship on their houses, producing mouldings, paneling and other details that

PLATE 70: *Hildreth House, Marietta*

[110]

put to shame most of the work that is done today. The jerry builder was then unheard of, homes were built to live in, not for speculative purposes, and the builder took a pride in his work that permitted him to do nothing but the best that his tools and his ability made possible.

COLONEL JOSEPH BARKER

Among the earliest of Ohio's master builders, and probably the first, was Colonel Joseph Barker, who came to Marietta in 1789, the year following the settlement of that oldest of Ohio towns. Barker was born September 9, 1765, at New Market, Rockingham County, New Hampshire. In 1774 his family moved to Amherst, New Hampshire, where the boy, after a few years of study at Exeter Academy, joined them when fourteen or fifteen years of age, and worked for a year or two with his father at the carpenter's trade. Leaving Amherst he went to New Ipswich where he perfected himself in his trade, "becoming a skillful architect," and in 1788 he worked as a journeyman carpenter on the meeting house at New Boston.

He married in 1789 and left Amherst in September of that year for the long journey to Marietta. We learn that in 1793 he removed from that settlement to Stone's Garrison at Belpre, fourteen miles down the Ohio River, to avoid an epidemic of smallpox. A permanent home was established by Barker, in 1795, at Wiseman's Bottom, a short distance up the Muskingum Valley above Marietta, and there he later built for himself a brick house that still stands in an excellent state of preservation, and practically unchanged in appearance. Two years after settling here, a fire in the cabin which he used as a shop and store room caused him to remove his business to Marietta where he built houses for many of the townspeople, and planned the courthouse that was built in 1822.

The most distinguished of Barker's clients was Harman Blennerhassett, for whom he built "the splendid mansion" where that ill-fated gentleman entertained Aaron Burr and his accomplished

PLATE 71: *Exchange Hotel, Harmar (Marietta). Built about 1831*

daughter, Theodosia. Here were planned details of the expedition that led to Burr's trial for treason, and wrecked the lives and fortunes of both men and their families. No trace remains of the beautiful house where the Blennerhassetts lived such an idyllic life before the advent of Aaron Burr. Drunken soldiers looted it, fire gutted it, and floods washed away what men and fire failed to destroy.

This house (built 1799-1800), consisted of a main building fifty-two feet long by thirty feet wide, with two dependencies connected with it by curving passageways. One of these housed the servants, the other was devoted to Blennerhassett's library and laboratory, where he spent much of his time in scientific research. The house was said to have cost $40,000.00, in addition to which $20,000.00 was expended on the surrounding grounds.

In spite of the large amount of construction attributed to Barker, it is difficult to identify his work today with any degree of certainty. The house which he built for his own occupancy at Wiseman's Bottom is of course authentic, and the similarity of design and detail in this and several other buildings in Marietta seems to warrant their attribution to him. Among these is the Hildreth House (Plate 70) which was built about 1824 and has a doorway quite like that of the house at Wiseman's Bottom. On both houses a similar use is made of blind arches. The old Exchange Hotel (Plate 71) in Harmar, on the west bank of the Muskingum River, has a similar doorway, and above it are triple windows like those in the Hildreth House. The Levi Barber House, built about 1828, has a similar doorway with triple windows above it.

The Hildreth House, which must have been a show place of early Marietta, bears evidence of the ship carpenter's craft in the form of anchors carved on one of the mantels. This house was built for Dr. Samuel P. Hildreth, who is said to have undertaken the project as a means of collecting a small fortune in unpaid bills which he had amassed during an epidemic of some sort in 1822 and 1823.

PLATE 72: *Mills House, Marietta. Built in 1820. Iron railing designed by Rufus E. Harte, a professor in Marietta College*

[114]

Dr. Hildreth was a scholar of note and made important contributions to the literature of science and history. It is to be hoped that his debtors responded generously to this opportunity for liquidating their accounts, thus freeing the good doctor somewhat from financial worries and leaving him with leisure and peace of mind to delve in his chosen fields of scholarly research.

The Exchange Hotel ceased long ago to function as a caravansary, but is still a rather impressive building. Like the old Mansion House on the other side of the river it has fallen to a low estate, but in spite of neglect, both reflect an aristocratic past. Both might yet be redeemed by the hand of an intelligent restorer.

The Mansion House, later known as the St. Charles Hotel (Plate 8), also has certain earmarks that suggest Barker's authorship or influence. The door has paneling that is similar to that used by him elsewhere, but on the other hand the columns are omitted and the elliptical fan light has given way to one that is circular. However, there is a certain "spikiness" in the design of both fan lights that suggests a relationship. The Exchange Hotel was built about 1831, though some assign an earlier date, and is said to have cost about $30,000.00. The Mansion House dates from 1835.

Joseph Barker was a man of superior ability as a builder and in addition possessed a knowledge of design that might well qualify him for the title of architect. He is in fact so designated in Hildreth's *Biographical and Historical Memoirs of the Early Settlers of Ohio* and is the only man in Marietta to be given that title, other craftsmen being mentioned as carpenters, cabinetmakers, and millwrights.

Meager data regarding other Marietta citizens with a flair for designing, indicate that a professor in the college, named Rufus E. Harte, in 1850 designed the second building erected for Marietta College; and he is also credited with the wrought-iron railing at the entrance of the near-by Mills House (Plate 72). This is the

PLATE 73: *Henry House, Parma. Built in 1850-57*

finest of the old Marietta houses and was built in 1820 for a postmaster of the town, named Wilcox. The portico was added and other changes made at a later date, probably about 1840.

John Delafield, Jr., is credited with having designed the old St. Luke's Church, a beautiful example of the Greek Revival, which was demolished long ago. As yet no evidence has been found that makes it possible to assign to him other old structures of the city.

Joseph Barker added to his other achievements the art of boat building, and was employed by Blennerhassett to construct the flotilla with which he and Aaron Burr planned to transport their famous or infamous expedition down the river. These boats were built on the banks of the Muskingum River, a short distance from its mouth. Had not President Jefferson sent Federal officers to look into the mysterious happenings on Blennerhassett Island, these Barker-built boats might have played a sinister part in bringing about momentous changes in the history of our nation.

ROBERT W. HENRY

An excellent example of the Classic Revival house stands as a landmark on the Wooster Pike at Parma, a short distance south of Cleveland. Four Doric columns carry the heavy entablature of the two-story central portion of the house across the portico which is its distinguishing feature. A peculiar variant in the detail of these columns is found in the use of a twelve-sided section instead of the customary flutings of the Doric order. This produces an effect that is, at a little distance, quite like that of a fluted column. A flat hipped roof covers this portion of the house (Plate 73).

At either side is a one-story wing with a gable roof which terminates against a brick wall. This is carried up to a horizontal coping level with the ridge. The wings also have porticos identical in design with that on the main block, excepting in height. A heavy dentil course is the one ornamental feature of the entablature.

The house was built by Robert W. Henry on a farm which he purchased in 1843. Family records show that he was seven years in building it, and that he secured his plans from published designs.

Robert's father, John Henry, brought his family to Cleveland in 1818 from Naples, Ontario County, New York, when the boy was seven years old. Here in 1823 the father died. Robert was "bound out" to a carpenter named Henry L. Nobles, with whom he remained as an apprentice until he became of age, afterward remaining with him for some time as a foreman.

Giving up this position, he worked at his trade on his own account for some twelve years when he removed to Parma. Here he operated his farm of one hundred and twenty-five acres and also followed his trade until 1885 when he retired, and died in 1900.

Stucco Ceiling, Farwell House, Hudson

PART III

SOURCES OF DESIGN

PLATE 74: *Sunbury Tavern (Hopkins House), Sunbury. The gallery adds a decidedly southern atmosphere to the place. From it Henry Clay once delivered a speech.*

PART III: SOURCES OF DESIGN

THE statement has been made elsewhere that the early builders were deeply indebted to books of design for help in preparing their plans. Numerous instances may be cited in which so close a correspondence is seen between existing examples of their work and designs published in books, that were owned by builders of the period, as to make quite certain the assumption that such publications were their actual source of inspiration.

This is illustrated in the cornice and frieze (Plate 75) of the Hopkins House (Plate 74) at Sunbury, which correspond closely to the design (Plate 77) for an "Eave Cornice" shown on Plate XXXV of Asher Benjamin's *The Architect, or Practical House Carpenter,* except that the guilloche is simplified and the cornice mouldings have been somewhat modified.

The portico of the Matthews House (Plate 11) at Zanesville might very well have been reproduced from Plate 52 of Minard Lafever's *The Modern Builder's Guide* (Plate 76) or Plate 11 of Asher Benjamin's *Practice of Architecture,* both of which reproduce details of the Doric Order from the temple of Minerva at Athens.

To be sure, these details might be secured from any illustrated work on classic architecture, but the fact that the books quoted were published for the definite purpose of providing source material for builders would make it seem rational to assume that the designers of the two buildings in question were in possession of these or similar books of design. These builders were not trained archaeologists or architects, but craftsmen dependent upon textbooks for such knowledge as was not acquired during their apprenticeship, or from practical experience on their jobs.

It is not to be supposed that the design books were used solely for literal copying; rather they were sources of suggestion, and the builders did as any other designers would do, modified and adapted the suggestions to suit themselves and the requirements of the job under construction.

Many details were doubtless learned by the builders while apprentices and became part of their stock in trade. Details of mouldings may well have been perpetuated by means of the knives of moulding planes, which were treasured possessions and descended from father to son so long as the steel survived the wear and tear of sharpening. However, with the change of fashion from Colonial to Classic Revival we find the delicate, early mouldings quite generally abandoned for the simpler, bolder forms which Jefferson copied from Palladio, forms which seem less appropriate for wood than the marble for which they were originally designed.

Habit and tradition go far in developing design, and it is most likely that in the majority of instances, after the owner or builder had made a crude plan for the proposed house, determining the approximate size of rooms, location of doors, windows, and fireplaces, the details were worked out as the job progressed, the builder drawing on such knowledge and books as he possessed, and running such mouldings as his kit of tools made possible. It must be assumed, of course, that he took pride in his work sufficient to make him delight in giving individual touches to each piece of work that came his way, and providing surprises here and there for his clients by the introduction of convenient cupboards, bits of ornament, decorative paneling, and other details that lend so much variety and interest to the old houses. Originality was not allowed too much license, else we should not find such close adherence to classic forms and details; still we must not suppose these men to have been slavishly bound to tradition for, despite the general uniformity of types, we rarely find two houses of the period identical in detail. The fertility of invention displayed in "ringing the changes" on stereotyped classical motifs is truly amazing.

PLATE 75: *Sunbury Tavern (Hopkins House). The details of cornice and frieze are so like those shown on the accompanying plate by Asher Benjamin that we may well assume the builder made use of this design, changing it to suit his needs.*

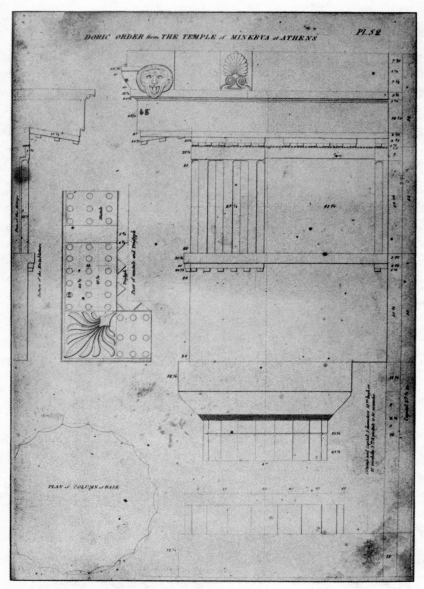

PLATE 76: *The Modern Builders' Guide (Plate 52), by Minard Lafever, New York, 1833. This shows the Doric Order from the Temple of Minerva at Athens, which was evidently taken from this or some other engraving, as the inspiration for the portico of the Matthews House, Zanesville (Plate 11)*

[124]

Certain details, that seem to be quite definitely localized, offer tempting opportunity for tracing the lines of immigration. Take for instance the four-lobed rosette that is cut through blocks on the frieze of a doorway (Plate 129) near North Bristol, in Trumbull County. It forms a most effective bit of ornament, the shadows in the perforations being much stronger than those on carving. Curiously enough this design, which is of rare occurrence, is found on a mantel in the Ruggles House at Columbia Falls, Maine, and there it is also pierced like a stencil, but through thin wood laid over a background of mahogany, thus producing the effect of dark pattern against a light ground by means of dark wood instead of shadow.

The mere fact that ornament of such similar character exists in places so widely separated would mean little perhaps were it not that it offers possible opportunity for following up the quest of this chapter. It may be quite significant indeed, for we know that the pioneers of this particular section of Ohio came from New Hampshire, which is not overly remote from Maine. What connection the builders of those two districts of New Hampshire and Maine may have had, or how this particular decorative motif reached the Western Reserve of Ohio, may never be known, but an interesting field for imagination is opened, and it may be that someone with time and means as well as imagination may eventually enter that field and reap a valuable harvest of facts regarding the journeys of our early builders.

The dilapidated little cottage (Plate 79) near Wellington shows definite Greek inspiration in the pierced fretwork of the frieze and the crude, carved anthemions which enrich the pilasters that flank the door. A similar use of the anthemion motif is suggested for a mantel pilaster on Plate 87 of Lafever's *Modern Builder's Guide* (Plate 78). Another house (Plate 80) near Wellington, and one at Ashland (Plate 81) have the anthemion repeated at top and bottom of the pilasters. In each instance the interpretation is quite crude. The three houses are not far apart, suggesting the possibility of a common origin.

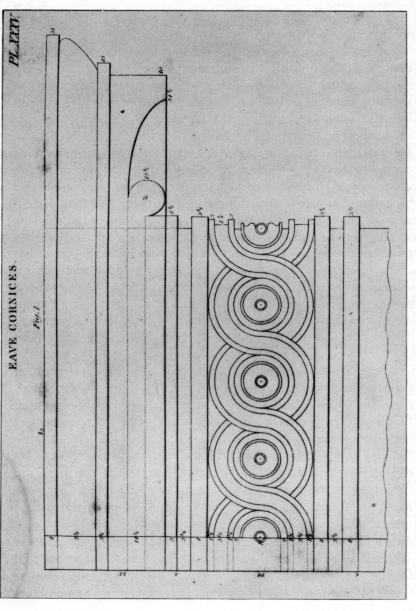

PLATE 77: "*The Architect, or Practical House Carpenter*" (Plate XXXV), by Asher Benjamin, Boston, 1848. Note close resemblance between this design and the cornice of Hopkins House, Sunbury (Plate 75)

The smokehouse (Plate 82) on the Renick-Young farm, Mount Oval, near Circleville, may be traced directly to Virginia, as it should be, for the Renicks came from the Old Dominion. Just what were the antecedents of this attractive little building may not be known, but certain it is that the open diamond pattern in the brickwork is to be found on various buildings in Virginia, including Bremo on the James and Barboursville in Orange County, both of which, by the way, were designed by Thomas Jefferson.

Ohio's early architecture was largely derivative, the pioneers having been far more concerned with housing themselves comfortably than with conducting experiments in architectural design. Fashions in architecture were already set in the east; the English Georgian had long since been simplified and adapted to the needs of the American Colonists; Charles Bulfinch and Samuel McIntire of Massachusetts were following the lead of the Brothers Adam; and Thomas Jefferson of Virginia was developing a highly formal style from the classic architecture of Rome, which he worked out with mathematical precision from the publications of Andrea Palladio, sixteenth century architect of Vicenza, Italy.

Ohio began to build seriously about the time that Mr. Jefferson's Classic Revival was at flood tide but, although it built largely in the current mode (Plates 12, 27, 48), we find that the older styles as well were commonly drawn upon (Plates 29, 33, 56). Most significant and interesting is the distinction between northern and southern types of the seaboard as they are reflected in the corresponding portions of Ohio. The low, compact farmhouse of Massachusetts and Connecticut, with its white clapboards and green shutters, is the characteristic type in the northern part of the state, although the more well-to-do families, especially in the towns, added to their social prestige by building with brick and stone, brick being the more usual of the two materials. Chimneys were built within the walls to conserve heat, ceilings were low for the same reason, and hallways were usually small, serving only as a means of communication between rooms.

PLATE 78: *"The Modern Builders' Guide"* (Plate 87), by Minard Lafever, New York, 1833. Note resemblance between ornament at top of pilaster panel and that on pilasters of house near Wellington (Plate 80)

Southern Ohio reflects the manners of the south. Brick was used more commonly, following the custom of Tidewater Virginia which is rich in clay suitable for brickmaking. The prevailing warm weather suggested the desirability of high ceilings. Hallways were made wide as well as high and stretched from front to back of the house, inducing currents of air that made them the most comfortable, hence the most used rooms in summer time. These features we find reproduced in the better class of houses in southern Ohio.

The classic colonnades of Mr. Jefferson's architectural fashion had become so universally popular that we can not regard them as peculiar to either north or south. The white columns of Greece and Rome were made features of all manner of buildings, domestic, secular, and religious, adding a touch of stateliness and dignity to innumerable village streets.

We miss in southern Ohio the dominating, white church spire of New England. The Virginians and Marylanders were avowedly devotees of the soil. They had few towns, and were satisfied that the towns should be few. They lived on vast plantations, and the "great house" of the plantation was the center of social life, instead of the village and the church as in New England. Hence we do not find the churches of Virginia and Maryland on the village green, overshadowing everything about them; instead we find them at the crossroads where they are accessible from neighboring plantations. Here the great families met for worship, but their social, intellectual, and political life centered elsewhere.

The courthouse was much more essential in the southern scheme of things. Sessions of court and of the State Assembly, rather than church meetings, dominated social life. Philadelphia, Annapolis, and Williamsburg were society centers of the states that fed immigrants to southern Ohio; and in Maryland and Virginia at least, when social life was not centered at the capitals during legislative sessions, it took the form of endless visits, parties, and balls at the great houses of the plantations.

PLATE 79: *House near Wellington, Lorain County*

PLATE 80: *House near Wellington. This and the pilaster from a house at Ashland show a strong family resemblance to the ornament on Plate 87 from Lafever's "Modern Builder's Guide." (Plate 78)*

PLATE 81: *House at Ashland—Detail of Pilaster*

[132]

Something of this tradition is reflected in southern Ohio, though in a minor key. The old aristocratic life was fading; the people who came west over the mountains were as a whole not of the patrician class; they bought small farms instead of vast plantations; the need for protection and companionship, as well as the need for centers where they might buy and sell, naturally resulted in the establishment of numerous towns. And so we find southern Ohio developing somewhat in the manner of New England, with small towns and small farms. Although there were great rivers, these were inland waterways and could not bring ships directly to the planter's private wharf as was the case in Tidewater. The great self-sustaining plantation was a thing of the past; farmer, merchant, and craftsman were mutually dependent; the industrial age was beginning.

The distinctions between the architecture of northern and southern Ohio will be understood more clearly perhaps by comparing the examples of each that are shown in the illustrations. The New England influence is seen in Plates 19, 20, 21, 22, 36, 37, 48, 56, 87, 88, 89, 90, 98. Southern characteristics, on the other hand, are more evident in Plates 2, 6, 9, 15, 23, 27, 44, 74, 102, 122.

Details of the Old Stone House (Plates 83, 100) at McConnelsville are quite obviously traceable to the Brothers Adam of England. The oval sunbursts and rectangular panels carved on the lintels of windows, not only of the first and second stories, but of the basement as well, give an air of striking distinction to this unusual house. The masonry shows excellent craftsmanship in the cutting and tooling, but unfortunately the stone of lintels and sills is weathering badly, and the ornament of the sills, which echoes that of the lintels, is nearly obliterated in places.

Little information is available regarding the history of this house except that it was built by an Englishman named Richardson, some say in 1838, while others believe it to be much older. It was used for many years as a tavern, with the barroom in the base-

PLATE 82: *Renick-Young—Smokehouse*

ment, access being gained to this presumably popular department of the hostelry by means of outside stone steps on both front and side. When the present owners purchased the house in 1905 they found the front door in the basement, built into the coal bin. This was replaced and the old kitchen fireplace was restored. The crane was found hanging in its place and the andirons were rescued from a heap of débris. At the same time a sink, cut from a large block of rough stone, was removed to make way for a more effective, though less picturesque fixture. The house as a whole is well worthy of careful study.

The pediment of an old bank building in Marietta has a drilled leaf ornament that may have been taken from Plate 26 in Asher Benjamin's *American Builder's Companion*. Comparison of plate and engraving (Plates 84, 85) makes this quite clear. Other details, such as the Ionic capitals, indicate that this was the work of a builder possessed of exceptional skill and knowledge.

The crude, applied fret found so commonly on buildings of the late Greek Revival period, may well be attributed to the plates published by Asher Benjamin. Two examples that are especially convincing as evidence of such origin are on the doorway of the Kennedy House near Aurora (Plate 88) and the two doorways of the Claridon Church (Plate 87) both of which are almost identical with the design reproduced in Plate 86. To be sure the side lights and the block above the cornice are omitted, as is the fret panel from the church doors, but in the latter case atonement has been made by repeating the fret on the three great pilasters of the façade.

A curious feature of this and other churches of the period, notably the one at Atwater (Plate 115), is the introduction of the pointed arch in windows of a design that is in other ways of classic inspiration. These windows reflect the approach of a Gothic Revival which, at a slightly later date closed the classic episode and begat a numerous family of weird churches, and other buildings as well, on which scrawny, emaciated buttresses, pinnacles, tracery, battlements and other pseudo-Gothic masonry details were wrought from barn boards and scantling by carpenters who were intended by Nature for brilliant careers as makers of stage scenery.

The early architecture of Ohio is so largely derivative, so largely a transplanting from eastern sources, and possesses so little that can be called its own, excepting the individuality and originality displayed in adapting old forms and details to new conditions and needs, that one of the real pleasures to be derived from its study is that of tracing its origins. Our early Ohio architecture differs from its prototypes chiefly in the simplification and ingenious interpretation of its details. In these we see reflected the hardships and penury of frontier life, the struggles of untutored minds with problems but half understood, the versatility born of necessity. If we will study the old structures with full recognition of the social, cultural, industrial, and financial handicaps under which those early builders labored, we must give them high praise for their achievement.

PLATE 83: *House at McConnelsville. The lintels and sills have most un-usual carving in low relief that shows a definite Adam inspiration.*

[137]

PLATE 84: *Bank of Marietta—Detail of façade. Built in 1831. The bed mould, under the modillions, has a drilled leaf ornament much like that shown on the Asher Benjamin plate reproduced here on Plate 85*

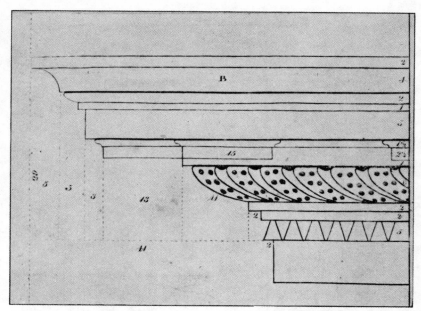

PLATE 85: *Asher Benjamin's "The American Builder's Companion" (Plate 26, Design B), Boston, 1816. Compare the drilled ornament with that shown on the bed mould of pediment on Bank of Marietta.*

PLATE 86: *From "The Architect, or Practical House Carpenter" (Plate XXVIII), by Asher Benjamin, Boston, 1848. Note resemblance between this design and doorways of Congregational Church at Claridon (Plate 87) and the Kennedy House near Aurora (Plate 88)*

PART IV
DWELLINGS

PLATE 87: *Church at Claridon, erected 1834. Compare detail with design by Asher Benjamin on Plate 86*

PART IV: DWELLINGS

THE dwelling, prior to the Civil War, was comparatively simple in plan and equipment. It lacked most of the conveniences that today are considered essential, and which are responsible for a large part of our building investment. The completed house prior to about 1875 was equivalent to the shell only of the modern house. There was no plumbing, no bathroom, no sewer or water pipes, no central heating plant with ducts or pipes to distribute the heat, no electric wiring system or lighting fixtures, no telephone connections, no iceless refrigeration, no incinerators. The completed house was indeed merely a shell, judged by our present-day standards.

The basement floor was usually of earth, though a few of the elect did pave it with brick or slabs of stone. The driveway outside may have been graveled, but the use of concrete for that purpose was as yet unheard of.

Convenience of arrangement for the housewife's benefit was given scant thought, the rooms being arranged according to convention or to suit the ideas of the builder rather than to economize the energies and steps of the housekeepers. The average large house of the north had a rather narrow central hall running from front to back, with two rooms on either side. The smaller house was more apt to have a small hall at one side connecting with the various rooms. The stairs were usually in the hallway although sometimes they disappeared mysteriously through space between other rooms.

In addition to the main block of the house, an L was quite likely to amble aimlessly until it had accumulated under its roof the kitchen, an assortment of pantries, a woodhouse, milk room, and possibly even the dining room itself. Bedrooms were sometimes provided under the low roof of the L for the accommodation of farm hands and other "help."

PLATE 88: *Kennedy House, Aurora*

[144]

This description is applicable more especially to the houses in small towns and rural districts. In the cities, and sometimes in the small towns as well, houses were crowded on narrow lots and up to the sidewalk, with stoops infringing on the rights of pedestrians. Little or no space was left between the houses for ventilation or light. With all the vast Northwest Territory to spread over, this niggardliness in Ohio's house sites can be explained only as the persistence of a primitive tendency to huddle into compact groups for social purposes and for greater protection against common enemies. The latter motive may have been justified here so long as Indians roamed the forests.

The great variety in house types and architectural details found in Ohio is readily understandable when we think of the varied origins, geographically and socially, of the early settlers, yet even then it is surprising, for the greater number of old Ohio houses were built within a period of thirty or forty years, that is from the end of the second decade of the nineteenth century, when prosperity made substantial building possible, until the outbreak of the Civil War brought that era to a close.

The very earliest crude structures had been, of course, replaced or remodeled as soon as means permitted, and the later ones were in turn obliterated as commercial and industrial growth raised property values in the towns that were blessed, or otherwise, by prosperity. In the smaller towns and in the rural districts, where financial considerations have not dictated such destruction, numerous interesting examples of the early architecture still remain, witnesses to the skill and the versatility of their builders.

The little cottage at Richfield (Plate 89) is reminiscent of those early New England cottages that met the needs of family expansion by the addition of a "lean-to," the "lean-to" having become here an integral part of the house. Its roof line still recalls the delightful sweep that is so admired in many an old house of the east. The low windows under the cornice were concealed, in some of the more

PLATE 89: *House at Richfield*

sophisticated later houses, behind grilles of wood or iron which became quite dominant decorative features of the design . (See Plates
46, 161-166.)

A low cottage of unusual character is shown on the next plate
(90). The simple composition, of a central recessed porch with
flanking pavilions, all pulled together by a low-pitched hip roof, is
in keeping with the more pretentious Swift House that formerly
stood near Vermillion (Plates 91-93, and 147).

Quite in contrast with these houses of northern Ohio is the definitely southern character of the house between Chillicothe and
McArthur (Plate 94). The upper gallery, with its wooden rail
is so essentially in the spirit of countless buildings in Virginia and
Maryland as to seem almost out of place in even the southern part
of Ohio. Rather exotic too is the little three-story building (Plate
95) that faces the levee of the Ohio River at Portsmouth. The
recessed porches, distinguished by Doric columns and entablatures,
and by simple iron handrails, give to this structure a very definite
claim on our attention, a claim that is enhanced by the local tradition that it was for a time the childhood home of Julia Marlowe.

An ingenious treatment of masonry is seen on the brick cottage
at Madison, Lake County (Plate 96). Recessed panels, on either
side of the doorway, frame in the windows and give a distinguished
effect to an otherwise commonplace front. The lattice porch also
adds materially to the effect, though it is questionable whether it
formed part of the original design. The attractiveness of this house
was destroyed not long after the photograph was taken by a coating
of stucco.

Greater sophistication is seen on the façade of the Brown House
at North Bloomfield. This is divided into three panels by pilasters
carrying an entablature, the architrave of which is cut away to form
low, flat arches. In the dining room is still to be seen the original
bake oven, concealed behind a hinged panel beside the fireplace;
and one of the bedrooms has on the walls the original grey, pastoral
paper, which came in square sheets instead of rolls.

PLATE 90: *House near Windsor*

This house was built in 1815-1816 by Ephraim Brown who, in 1814, came to Trumbull County where he owned 16,000 acres of land, purchased from the Connecticut Land Company. Most of these extensive holdings were sold by him to friends and relatives who afterward settled here. Mr. Brown came from Westmoreland, New Hampshire, his wife from Windham, Connecticut, and the home which they built for themselves in the Western Reserve has never passed out of the family. It is the finest of a group of apparently related houses scattered for some miles along the road north of Warren (Frontispiece and Plate 97).

A similarity of type in all this group suggests a common source of design, but at this writing no information regarding the identity of the builder or builders has been found, unless that credit can be given to Mr. Brown himself. Details of another house in this group are illustrated on Plates 129 and 130.

The simple dignity of the old Ohio houses is well exemplified in the house at Atwater, shown on Plate 98. The proportions are good, the detail of the pediment is refined, and the front entry partially echoes this detail in a minor key. The lattice is presumably a later innovation, replacing columns that originally supported the pediment. This assumption may well explain the clumsy structure beneath the entablature, which can scarcely be attributed to the same hand that worked out other details of the house.

The Cox House (Plate 99) at Dresden, Muskingum County, in central Ohio, is quite different from the preceding examples of Western Reserve design. The stone quoins rather overemphasize the corners and the doorway, while above the latter is a heavy lintel that quite dominates the façade. An enormous rosette is carved on the key panel and on each end are four-lobed rosettes, curiously like those that have been noted on the doorway at North Bristol (Plate 129).

Stepped gables and an elaborate cast iron fence are the salient features of the Mumaugh House at Lancaster, shown on Plate 101.

PLATE 91: *Joseph Swift House (formerly at Swift's Hollow), near Vermillion. Built in 1840-1; burned in 1923*

It was built about 1820, by a banker named Michael Geraghty, in front of a much older structure that still forms a rear wing. The builder is supposed to have been Daniel Sifford, who is credited with many of the old Lancaster houses. The Mumaugh House stands in an historic environment, being across the street from the boyhood home of John and William Tecumseh Sherman, and the home of General Thomas Ewing, father-in-law of General Sherman, and Secretary of the Treasury during the administration of William Henry Harrison. It was in this latter house that Sherman is said to have planned the march to the sea.

The house was sold to John A. Mumaugh in 1826 and remained in the family until 1931 when it was willed to the city of Lancaster as a meeting place for local women's clubs, and to house collections of the Historical Society.

The Scioto Valley is another section of Ohio that is rich in history, in agricultural lands, in archaeological remains of prehistoric populations, and in early architecture. On the banks of this river, where it is crossed by the old National Road, stands Columbus, the present capital of the state. Further down the stream is the first capital, Chillicothe, and at its mouth, where the waters are poured into the Ohio, is Portsmouth. These three cities and the many little towns between are rich in architectural reminders of the past. The house at Waverly (Plate 102) is typical of the better class of farm houses in this region. It is built of brick with stone trimmings, and has but the slightest hint of a cornice to cap its walls, a tendency in the south that contrasts with the overly heavy cornices common in the Western Reserve.

The Scioto Valley is a happy hunting ground for the student of early architecture; in fact this is true of most portions of the state that were easily accessible to the pioneers and that possessed soil sufficiently rich to tempt settlers. The towns along the Ohio are as a rule possessed of more or less architectural interest, though prosperity with increasing real estate values has been responsible for the

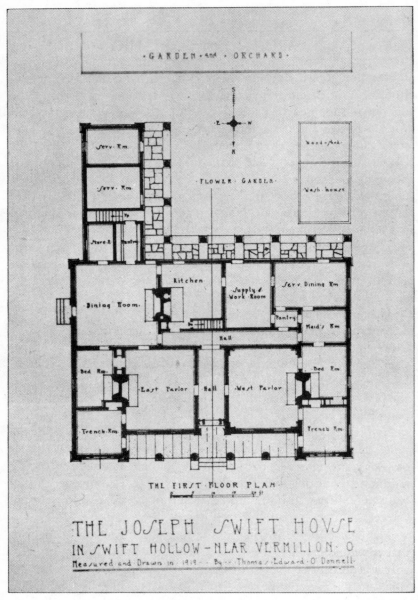

PLATE 92: *Plan of the Joseph Swift House. (Reproduced by courtesy of Thomas E. O'Donnell from "The Western Architect")*

[152]

destruction of most of the early buildings. Cincinnati, for instance, has practically nothing of architectural value that recalls the better element of its early society, the Sinton-Taft House (Plate 44) being the one outstanding example that remains.

THE SINTON-TAFT HOUSE, CINCINNATI

One of the finest of Ohio's early houses is in Cincinnati, the Sinton-Taft House, which was bequeathed to the city by the Hon. and Mrs. Charles P. Taft as a museum to house their collection of art works. It is now called the Taft Museum.

Little is known regarding the architect or builders of the house, or indeed as to the exact date of its construction. The most definite information is contained in a letter addressed to the original owner, Martin Baum, which reads as follows:

Mr. M. Baum   Cincinnati, Aug. 23, 1820.
Sir:

I will assume for you at Bank $62,000 for the following property, to wit, Front and Sycamore Streets property, Market and Broadway Streets property, New house and materials with the nine acres on which it stands, with Deer Creek and Hill property. . . . . And will close the thing with you tomorrow and relieve you from all your bank debts to that amount. If any person will make you a better offer, close with them without waiting to consult me.

Respectfully your friend,
(Signed) W. LYTLE.

An accompanying list of Mr. Baum's assets and liabilities contained item: "Nine acres of land this side of Deer Creek and new house thereon. $30,000." This was the place we are now considering.

The letter specifies "new house and materials" which suggests that it was still under construction or but recently completed.

It was deeded to the United States Bank in 1826, and three years later was purchased by Nicholas Longworth. David Sinton purchased it in 1869 and from him it descended to his daughter, Mrs. Charles P. Taft.

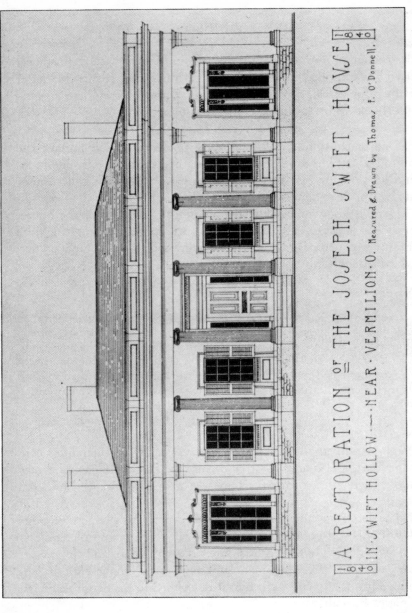

PLATE 93: *Front elevation of the Joseph Swift House.* (*Reproduced by courtesy of Thomas E. O'Donnell from "The Western Architect"*)

Local tradition names as the architect James Hoban, who designed the White House at Washington, but no records have been found to substantiate this claim. Better grounds exist for attributing it to Benjamin Henry Latrobe, who was Surveyor of Public Buildings under Presidents Jefferson and Madison. Latrobe is known to have spent some time at Pittsburgh and in the introduction to *The Journal of Latrobe* it is stated that, "While at Pittsburgh, he designed several private buildings that were erected there or in the immediate vicinity. Also for other places. Among these last were the residences of Henry Clay at Lexington and Governor Taylor at Newport." Beyond this the identity of the designer is but a matter of surmise.

The house has been carefully restored in preparation for its use as a museum, and various Victorian details including the front doorway, have been removed, the exterior restorations being based on a colored print of the house dated 1857.

Mural paintings of excellent quality, found on the walls of the entrance hall, have been recovered from under many coats of wall paper and varnish. These include eight romantic landscapes and four overdoors, two of the latter representing bowls of flowers and fruit, the other two American eagles. These murals were painted by Robert S. Duncanson, who worked in Cincinnati from 1843 to 1851.

THE CURTIS-DEVIN HOUSE, MT. VERNON

Drawings and specifications for the early buildings of Ohio, and in fact of the country at large, were so casual and crude that scant significance was attached to them after the job was finished; there was little reason for their preservation, so few examples are to be found today. For this reason exceptional interest attaches to a set of existing contracts that are given in full in the Appendix.

The original owner of the house, which still stands at Mount Vernon, was Henry B. Curtis, who came to Mount Vernon from Vermont where he was born in 1799. In 1829 he built a brick

PLATE 94: *House between McArthur and Chillicothe. The southern influence is unmistakable*

PLATE 95: *This unique house in Portsmouth faces the levee of the Ohio River. It is said to have been the childhood home of Julia Marlowe*

PLATE 96: *This little brick house at Madison is distinguished by the recessed panels which group the windows. Shortly after the photograph was taken, a coating of stucco completely ruined the effect of the house*

house opposite the site of the present one. The earlier structure was a beautiful example of Colonial architecture, with a front door framed with side lights and fan light, above which was a Palladian window.

The present house was begun in 1834 and completed a year or two later. In 1850 alterations were made in conformity with the fashionable Greek Revival, at which time the balconies were added to the front and the marble mantels were removed from the double parlor.

This house presents a definite illustration of the manner in which builders of the time took their designs from the plates of architectural publications. The contracts state specifically that the exterior entablature and the drawing-room mantels are to be made according to plates in Shaw's *Civil Architecture,* edition of 1831. Examination of the third edition, dated 1834 and preserved in the Library of Congress, shows that the builder worked very closely to the details specified.

There is a change in the numbering of plates in the two editions of Shaw's book, but Plate 56 in the later edition is without doubt the Plate 55 in the edition possessed by Mr. Curtis. This shows the Roman Ionic order from the Temple of Concord at Rome. Plate 57 in the earlier edition thus becomes 58 in the later, and shows the Corinthian order from the portico of the Pantheon at Rome.

Plate 74 of the 1834 edition seems to be the one referred to in connection with the parlor mantel design, for on it are shown two "Designs for Chimney Pieces," one of which has a simple entablature, supported by plain columns with Ionic capitals. The details are simple enough to be readily worked out in marble by good stone cutters such as the two men who came from England to the nearby town of Gambier to work on the buildings of Kenyon College. (See page 310 Appendix).

In view of the alterations made in 1850, it is difficult to determine just how closely Irvin and Armstrong followed the original specifications, though we may well infer that a man as meticulous as was Mr. Curtis in drawing his contracts would not permit deviations from them without good and sufficient cause. However, as the house stands today the modillions, which the owner was to have the privilege of omitting from the west cornice "if he sees proper," are missing on the other sides as well, while the dentils appear both on the horizontal and raking cornices. The frets moreover are not restricted to five in number, but appear above all the windows. Very little deviation is evident between the Shaw design and the remaining marble mantel, now in a bedroom on the second floor.

The huge scrolled acroteria that surmount the gables, and the balustrade at the eaves were doubtless added during the 1850 reconstruction, and the two-paned sash are also of later date.

THE JOSEPH SWIFT HOUSE, VERMILLION

A most unusual residence (Plates 91, 92, 93, 147) was built in 1840 and 1841 on the Vermillion River about seven miles south of the town of Vermillion. The owner, Joseph Swift, was a native of Williamstown, Massachusetts, his father having been a clergyman of that place and one of the founders of Williams College.

The broad recessed porch with its four Ionic columns, together with the flanking pavilions accented by their unusual French windows (Plate 147), gives to the house rare distinction. Details reflect strongly the spirit of the Greek Revival as illustrated in the books of Lafever.

The roof was crowned originally by a balustrade, that must have added much to its appearance, but this had disappeared long before the accompanying photograph was made.

According to family tradition a New York architect designed the house, and it was built by a Mr. Lang of Elyria. Framing timbers were gotten out locally while the whitewood trim was milled in Cleveland. The four Ionic columns of the porch and the carving on the French windows are said to have come from some place in

PLATE 97: *Ephraim Brown House, North Bloomfield*

[161]

PLATE 98: *House at Atwater*

New York State. This may explain the contrast between the detail of these features and the comparative crudity of other detail in the house, which was mostly in the form of rather coarse, jigsawed adaptations of the classic fret. Mouldings were fairly good in profile.

Extensive and well laid-out grounds surrounded the house which, because of the profusion of roses was called Rosedale.

Architects from far and near were attracted by the unusual character of the house, but its remote location led ultimately to its abandonment. In time it became known as the "Haunted House" and was regarded as fair game for all manner of vandalism. Roofs sagged, a column lay across the lawn, doors were torn from their hinges, walls were disfigured with names, and finally in 1923 it was burned, just as a movement was being started to purchase and restore it. With its passing, Ohio lost one of its rarest architectural treasures.

SHANDY HALL, UNIONVILLE

One of the oldest houses in the Western Reserve is Shandy Hall, the Harper homestead at Unionville. Its builder, Robert Harper, was a colonel in the War of 1812 and the youngest son of Captain Alexander C. Harper, whose family was one of the three first to settle in Ashtabula County.

Alexander Harper's life had been replete with the thrills of frontier life and Indian warfare, including a miraculous escape from death while a prisoner of the celebrated Mohawk chief, Captain Brant; and capture during the Revolution by the British, who imprisoned him for two years and eight months at Quebec.

Following his release in 1783 Captain Harper and his family returned to Harpersfield, New York, a town of which he had been one of the founders in 1770. He moved again in 1798 to the Western Reserve where, as leader of the little expedition, he gave the name of Harpersfield to the township in which they settled. After a summer of hardships Captain Harper contracted malarial

PLATE 99: *Cox House, Dresden*

fever, died September 10, 1798, and was buried in a section of log hollowed out for a coffin, on a sandy knoll which he himself had selected as a burial spot. This is now the old cemetery at Unionville and his grave, which was the first to be dug there, is said to be the oldest authentically marked burial place of a white man in the Western Reserve.

Captain Harper's widow, Elizabeth Bartholomew, carried on after his death with fortitude and resourcefulness that seem superhuman in view of the dangers and hardships that beset those early days. Starvation, wild animals, drowning, and other perils of the wilderness threatened her and her young family, but in spite of all she saw them grow up, marry and settle about her. The youngest son, Robert, in 1815 built the original house, the story and a half portion of Shandy Hall that faces the road. Here his mother spent her old age.

The house consisted of two rooms on the first floor, with a stairway between, and bedrooms in the second story. In 1825 or 1828 additions were made that completely surrounded the original structure excepting on the south side, or front. These additions are low lean-tos at both ends, each with a recessed porch in front, and a connecting link, which includes the dining room, across the back.

The exterior is covered with clapboards except for the recessed porches, where the walls are sheathed with wide boards as are the half gables above. If the house were ever painted, little evidence of it remains; instead the old boards have acquired the soft grey tone that comes with honorable age.

The wing at the west of the house contains a long, narrow room that was used originally as the owner's office, and adjoining this is his bedroom. Directly back of the main block are the "banquet hall" and kitchen, between which is a large chimney with a fireplace for each of these rooms and a third for a small one in the rear.

The banquet hall is the outstanding feature of the house. It is twenty-nine feet seven inches long by fourteen wide, with seven

PLATE 100: *The Old Stone House, McConnelsville. So called because it is only stone house in the town. Date of building is unknown*

feet nine inch side walls, and nine feet five inches height in the center of the low barrel-vaulted ceiling. A chair rail is carried around the room forming a dado, above which is hung a French scenic paper that is still in an excellent state of preservation. According to family tradition this paper was imported from France for a large hotel in Philadelphia, about 1830. For some reason it was never used there and was ultimately purchased in Buffalo by Colonel Harper and in 1835 was hung on the walls of this room (Plates 108, 109).

THE ALLEN HOUSE, KINSMAN

Features of unusual character are found in the Allen House (Plate 110) at Kinsman. The façade (Plate 111) is distinguished by the use of an order which recalls the lightness of touch common to English architecture of the late eighteenth century. Four pilasters with Ionic capitals are carried up the full two stories of the house, supporting a light and richly ornamented entablature with a pediment above.

The full entablature is returned on the sides of the house, but with none of the ornament except the cornice modillions. Flush matched siding is used on the front wall, serving to set off the architectural features, but the side walls are laid up with ordinary clapboards.

The doorway and the elliptical fan light above (Plate 112) are enframed by an Ionic order with fluted pilasters and an entablature with carved sunbursts on the frieze. Above the windows (Plate 113) is a frieze and cornice, and on the side casings is a simple fret that seems a little too coarse to be in scale with other ornament of the façade, but is nevertheless effective. Windows on the other walls are similar in design to those on the front but are without ornamentation.

Interior woodwork echoes that of the exterior in detail. The parlor was worked out with especial care, having Ionic pilasters as features flanking the openings, an ornamental entablature at the

PLATE 101: *Mumaugh House, Lancaster. Bequeathed for use of women's clubs, and a historical museum*

ceiling, and a mantel with twin colonnettes on each side and a frieze on which are repeated the sunbursts and other details of the front doorway (Plate 114).

The house was built in 1821 by Dr. Peter Allen, and was the birthplace of his grandson, Dudley Peter Allen, who became a most distinguished member of Cleveland's medical fraternity.

In 1903 Dr. Allen had the parlor woodwork removed from the Kinsman House and installed in his Cleveland residence. Ten years later it was again removed, this time to his estate on Mayfield Road in Cleveland Heights, where it still remains.

The interior trim throughout the old Allen House is unusually refined and delicate in detail, as is that of other houses in Kinsman, giving indisputable evidence of the exceptional skill and taste possessed by the town's pioneer builders.

THE KINSMAN HOUSES

Another house that well deserves attention is the Kinsman homestead that was built about 1820 to 1823, by Rebecca Perkins Kinsman, whose husband, John Kinsman, was founder of the town. He was among the largest landholders of the Western Reserve, and was a leading citizen of Trumbull County until his death in 1813. He brought his family from the east in 1804 and established a store or trading post designed to serve the entire Reserve. After living for a few years in a log house, he built the original Kinsman House that was destroyed by fire shortly after his death. This was replaced, on a site diagonally across the road, by the present dwelling whose doorway is shown here (Plate 150).

The interior trim resembles in many ways that of the Allen House, the mantels (Plate 114) being almost identical, differing only in minor details. An elliptical arch spans the hall at the foot of the stairs, its richly carved detail adding materially to the impression of richness which is given one upon entering.

The house was erected under the supervision of Mrs. Kinsman's son, John, by workmen from Lisbon, Connecticut, the master

PLATE 102: *Waverly, Pike County. Located in the rich Scioto Valley, this house is typical of those built by well-to-do farmers in the southern part of the state*

builder being a man named Smith. They did much work in the vicinity, including the Peter Allen House and that of Isaac Allen, the inn on the square, and a house for George Swift, who had married a daughter of the Kinsmans. All this work was executed between 1820 and 1830, but exact dates are peculiarly difficult to determine.

The same group of workmen built the church (1831-1832) after the design, so it is said, of the Old North Church in New Haven, Connecticut. Much of the cost of this building was borne by Madame Kinsman. This title of "Madame" was quite generally used to express the deference felt for her rare character by her frontier neighbors, and even the Indians are said to have shown equal respect by calling her "Sin-e-Qua."

This extraordinary woman showed great ability in handling the large estate left by her husband, combining business acumen with generosity. During the 1840's when the little Western Reserve College at Hudson (Page 55) seemed about to give up its struggle for existence, Madame Kinsman gave $6,000.00 for its relief, and induced her brother, General Simon Perkins of Warren, to do the same. Her message to him was, "We must not let that college down. You must give and I will give." This saved the college, which has since developed into Western Reserve University.

In recognition of that service the university still maintains the Perkins Chair of Physics, and a portrait of Rebecca Perkins Kinsman hangs in the office of the university president. She died in 1852 at the age of eighty-two.

Frederick, the youngest son of Madame Kinsman, was born at Kinsman in 1807. On the occasion of his marriage to his first cousin, Olive Douglas Perkins, her father General Simon Perkins gave to the young couple a corner of his home lot in Warren, on which they built the house shown on Plate 27. The only house in Warren comparable to it was the Quinby House (Plate 57). This latter place, which was torn down in 1931, was designed and built by a man named Isaac Ladd, who also constructed the woodwork for the original courthouse.

PLATE 103: *Curtis-Devin House, Mount Vernon. Built in 1834-36, by Henry B. Curtis. Remodeled about 1850, when balcony was added and house given definite feeling of Greek Revival*

PLATE 104: *Curtis-Devin House—Stairway*

[173]

PLATE 105: *Curtis-Devin House—Upper stairway*

[174]

PLATE 106: *Curtis-Devin House—Marble mantel. Copied from plate in Edward Shaw's "Civil Architecture." See page 318, Appendix*

PLATE 107: *House at Braceville, Trumbull County. The cornice consists of four projecting courses of bricks which form a "dog tooth" effect, and stop against stone corner blocks cut to the same profile.*

PLATE 108: *Shandy Hall, Unionville—Banquet hall. Part of addition that was built in 1825 or 1828*

[177]

PLATE 109: *Shandy Hall—French scenic paper in banquet hall. The paper was hung in 1835*

PLATE 110: *Allen House, Kinsman. Built in 1821*

PLATE III: *Allen House—Façade*

[180]

PLATE 112: *Allen House—Front Doorway*

[181]

PLATE 113: *Allen House—Front window*

[182]

PLATE 114: *Allen House—Mantel*

[183]

PART V
PUBLIC BUILDINGS

PLATE 115: *Congregational Church, Atwater. Begun in 1838; dedicated November 7, 1841*

PART V: PUBLIC BUILDINGS

THE construction of dwellings occupied the attention of Ohio's early builders to a very large extent, but they were called upon also to exercise their ingenuity on a goodly number of public buildings. First of course were the churches, especially in the northern part of the state, with its New England background. Those who settled the southern portion, apparently took their religion less seriously, as had their Virginia forebears. There are fewer old churches of architectural interest south of the National Road; while on the Western Reserve there is apt to be a plurality of churches in every town, no matter how small. In this connection it should not be forgotten that in New England the community life centered about the town, and the town in turn had as its center the church. The white church with its spire pointing heavenward served not only as a meeting place for religious services, but was also the center of social, and, to an extent, of political life. The more southerly states, such as Maryland and Virginia, were differently constituted. Vast estates took the place of small farms, and towns were almost unknown. Each plantation was a self-sustaining community, sufficient unto itself. Social life centered around the "great house" of the plantation, and the church was placed at the crossroads where it was used for little else than the formal services of the Church of England.

Both south and north, a courthouse is to be found at every county seat, and here the Virginians and Marylanders were at their best. They took to politics and the law as New Englanders did to trade.

Of taverns and inns there were unlimited numbers in Ohio, especially along the stage routes and the great overland roads that carried the tide of immigration westward. These were not so different from the dwellings, but were a little more roomy. Then of course there were commercial buildings to house the merchants' stocks-in-trade, and there were school and college buildings.

Large numbers of these buildings have disappeared, having given way to rising property values and the demand for more commodious and up-to-date accommodations. This destruction has been especially rife in the cities, while in the smaller towns and the country, with less means available and less growth in population to demand change, the old buildings remain.

CHURCHES

Few if any churches are to be found in Ohio that equal in beauty the ones at Tallmadge (Plate 37) and Atwater (Plate 115). Both are outstanding examples that compare favorably with most of the New England churches. The Tallmadge church is quite consistently classical in design, but the one at Atwater has windows with pointed arches, an anachronism that frequently occurs.

Smaller churches like those at Twinsburg (Plate 116) and Streetsboro (Plate 36) are reasonably numerous, but rarely of such good proportions. St. Luke's (Plate 117) at Granville represents another type of Classic Revival. The church at Claridon has a most interesting cornice (Plate 87), but the belfry tower is less successful. The one at Freedom (Plate 118) is still less so, but the massive portico possesses considerable distinction.

THE MORMON TEMPLE

One of the most historic church buildings in Ohio, though not to be ranked among the most beautiful, is the temple (Plate 41) built by the Mormons at their early stronghold, Kirtland. Here Joseph Smith, Brigham Young, Sidney Rigdon, and other leaders in that organization of Latter Day Saints, established themselves and their followers. Here Mormonism gained the momentum that carried it across the continent and even to the Old World. The temple was built in response to "divine revelation," through profound spiritual devotion, personal sacrifice, and by the labor of all the community.

PLATE 116: *Congregational Church, Twinsburg. Built in 1848*

PLATE 117: *St. Luke's Episcopal Church, Granville*

[190]

Erection of a "grand temple" as a "lasting monument to Zion'
was determined upon following a "revelation to Joseph Smith, Jr.
on May 6, 1833." In the journal of Heber C. Kimball it is stated
that President Joseph Smith, Jr. was foreman in the quarry, "The
Presidency, high priest, and elders all alike assisting. Those who
had teams assisted in drawing the stone to the house. These all
laboring one day in the week, brought as many stones to the house
as supplied the masons through the whole week. We continued in
this manner until the walls of the house were reared. . . . The
committee who were appointed by revelation to superintend the
building of the house were, Hyrum Smith, Reynolds Cahoon, and
Jared Carter." The master builder was Joseph Bump who was given
each evening a special revelation from the Prophet, outlining his
duties for the following day.

The corner stone was laid July 24, 1833, and the temple was
dedicated March 27, 1836. Four days and nights of emotional
excitement followed. Thousands came from all over northern Ohio,
and Joseph Smith and Brigham Young were at the height of their
power. Smith communed with saints of old, including, according
to his statement, Moses, Elijah and Elisha. Young was seized with
the "gift of tongues" and preached a sermon which, though unin-
telligible to his hearers, was devoutly believed by them to be
couched in the language of inspiration. Many signs and wonders
were observed, including heavenly music in the air and a pillar of
fire which hovered over the temple.

The building is eighty feet in length by sixty in width, and three
stories high. The walls are built of rough stones covered with
cement, which is marked off in imitation of dressed masonry. The
first and second stories are occupied by auditoriums, having grouped
pulpits at each end, for the priesthoods of Aaron and of Melchis-
edec. These pulpits are in four tiers, rising toward the back, each
tier having seats for three priests. In front of the lower pulpit is a
drop leaf of walnut which, when raised, forms a table for the administration of the sacrament (Plates 42-43).

PLATE 118: *Church at Freedom. The belfry tower is not as successful in design as the portico*

Curtains attached to rollers on the ceiling provided means by which the pulpits could be separated and the pews be divided into four groups. This mechanism is still intact in the upper auditorium.

The woodwork, especially that of the pulpits (Plate 43), is well designed and excellently built. Despite the claims of divine revelation, it reflects the Greek Revival influence, fashionable at the time, especially in the use of the fret and guilloche, many variations of the former appearing in the trim. A free treatment of a flowing vine motif, on the casing of one of the large windows, is in striking contrast to the severely classical ornament used elsewhere.

The second and third floor vestibules open together through a light well, and the stairways rise at opposite ends with landings against the outside walls. The third floor is divided into classrooms, lighted by dormer windows.

The Mormon Temple is unique among church edifices, and well merits study for its architectural features and for the curious arrangement by which the auditoriums were adapted to requirements of the Mormon ritual.

TAVERNS

Of taverns there is no end. Several have already been noted (Plates 2 to 9). These differ but little from the houses of their vicinity. They are larger, and so far as the exterior is concerned might easily be mistaken for the homes of affluent townsmen.

There was a tendency, especially in the southern part of the state to build porches and galleries across the front similar to those common in the southern states. An example of this practice is seen on the Sunbury Tavern, now the Hopkins House, at Sunbury (Plates 74, 75), which has galleries on both stories that are given further mention on page 121. The house, or a part of it, was built in 1804 by Joe Adams on property owned by his father, Joel Adams, and is said to have been the first frame building erected in Sunbury.

Little reliable data is available regarding this interesting building, and so many changes and restorations have been made that it is

PLATE 119: *Hotel at Zoar*

difficult to determine its original form. Two apparently unrelated roofs in the rear suggest that early buildings may have been combined, and that the portico and possibly the main roof may have been later constructions.

The framework is of the sturdy kind common in pioneer construction. The lower floors are carried on logs hewn flat on the upper side, but otherwise left round, and in some instances with the bark remaining. Black walnut 4″ x 4″ studding has been uncovered in the course of restorations, and it is said that the siding is of that wood. Ordinary clapboard was used, excepting on the walls back of the porches where flush sheathing was substituted.

The stone flagging of the porch formerly served as a section of the street sidewalk, and the foot scrapers at the ends suggest that the town's folks were obliged to content themselves with mother earth or clay elsewhere along the way.

A semicircular stone mounting block (page 308), now preserved in the back yard as a curiosity, recalls the days of horseback riding and high carriages.

Within the house, in one of the front rooms, are still to be seen traces of the old bar with cupboards beside it in which were stored the bottles. The mantel in this same room retains somewhat of its former beauty, though much of the reeding which gave it distinction has been destroyed. The same ignorant vandalism is in evidence on the porch cornice where a painter was discovered by the owner in the act of cutting away the delicate dentils in order to save himself the trouble of painting them.

The second floor was divided originally into small rooms by means of movable partitions. These were fastened together by hooks, and could be removed and stowed away when on gala occasions a large floor was needed for dancing. Tradition tells of a certain New Year's ball for which a whole beef was cooked. Rain fell while the festivities were in progress, followed by intense cold which froze the wagon wheels so solidly in the mud that the merry-

PLATE 120: *Old hotel at Palmyra, Portage County. This was once an important coal mining center, hence the large inn; for many years used as a dwelling*

makers were compelled to remain until morning when the wheels could be chopped loose from the frozen ground. Years afterward one of the members of that storm-bound party used to point out to her children the spot, in a near-by log house, where nine girls slept or tried to sleep during what was left of that frigid night.

Sections of a 17½" baseboard are still to be seen in two of the bedrooms, evidently survivals of the old ballroom trim.

The cellar, which extends under only a portion of the house, has no floor other than the clay which Nature provided. From one end a small wine cellar extends under the portico floor and has stone shelves built into the wall, providing storage for the bottles whose contents cheered and doubtless inebriated the patrons of the inn.

The columns of the portico are spaced in a curiously irregular manner, the two middle ones being 9'-0" apart on centers, those at the left approximately 8'-0", and those at the right 9'-4½" and 9'-7", the widest spacing being at the extreme right. Thus the refinement of intercolumniation which is suggested on the left side is negatived by the carelessness displayed on the right.

The columns were turned from solid logs, were carefully fluted, and set on cut stone plinths. One column at the left and two at the right came to grief when crashed by runaway horses and have been replaced in a manner that effectually "shows up" the lack of architectural understanding in the average modern carpenter.

The Sunbury Tavern had its quota of distinguished guests in stagecoach days, among them having been Henry Clay and ex-Presidents Harrison and Hayes. Clay made a speech from the upper gallery.

The hotel at Zoar (Plate 119) reflects somewhat the spirit of the Germans from Württemberg who settled the town in 1817. Here in Stark County they established themselves on a tract of 5,500 acres and, shortly after their arrival, organized on a communistic basis, all property being held in common, although the families retained their integrity. Houses and vast barns were roofed with

PLATE 121: *Dunham Tavern, Cleveland. Built in 1842*

red tile and the entire town possessed an Old World atmosphere.

Inns of impressive size are sometimes found in towns so small that they seem quite inadequate as settings for hostelries as pretentious as the one at Palmyra (Plate 120). This particular town was at one time the center of an important coal field, the product of which, Palmyra lump, was famous throughout northern Ohio. With the exhaustion of the coal supply the town dwindled, leaving its three-story inn as a pathetic reminder of vanished prosperity.

THE DUNHAM TAVERN, CLEVELAND

Few buildings erected by the pioneers of Cleveland stand today. Like most large American cities, the demands of its industrial and commercial life, with the attendant rise of property values, have demanded their destruction. The dollar in America is crushing and deadly to anything that gets in its way.

One of the rare survivors from Cleveland's early days is the Dunham Tavern (Plate 121) which is the oldest building now standing on Euclid Avenue, and is said to have been the first one built on that road east of 55th Street. Its original owners were Rufus and Jane Pratt Dunham, who came in 1823 from Mansfield, Massachusetts, to the 140-acre farm that stretched north from Euclid Road to what is now Hough Avenue.

Here they spent many years of hard work and privation, sometimes with a larder limited to corn meal and potatoes. During one of these disheartening periods of food shortage, old friends arrived from Massachusetts and, in order that the guests might not suspect the grim poverty of the little household, Mrs. Dunham walked to the home of Elizabeth Ingersoll, three miles distant on the heights, and borrowed some salt pork and flour to liven up the menu.

There was spirit as well as dogged determination in those pioneer women, as we may infer from another incident that has come down among the family traditions. It seems that for a time the none too commodious log house was shared with another family, and one day the two housewives discovered that their "men folks" had gone away without filling the kitchen woodbox. Now it is quite possible that this had happened before for the women took the slight much more seriously than would seem necessary if it were only a slip of the memory. At any rate they apparently determined that this carelessness or laziness should not be casually overlooked, and calmly proceeded to go outdoors, set fire to the entire wood pile, and cook their meal beside it.

The husbands' comments were not recorded, but it is to be hoped that they saw the error of their way and profited permanently from this fiery hint.

The Dunhams were able in 1842 to replace the old log house with the present frame building; but in 1853 they deeded the place to Ben and John Welsh with "exactly 4 acres of land together with the tavern thereon and all barns and sheds used in connection with said Tavern House." It was still known as the "Old Jim Welsh Place" when in 1884 it was purchased by Dr. J. A. Stephens.

The old tavern was leased in 1932 by A. Donald Gray, landscape architect, who has endeavored to restore somewhat the original atmosphere, while using it partially as an office for his business and leasing the rest to others engaged in artistic pursuits.

The framework of the tavern is of heavy hewn timbers, put together with wooden pins and hand-wrought spikes. The first floor joists are also of hewn logs, and the rooms are separated by partitions of chestnut planks on which the plaster is laid over split lath.

A feature of the place was a water tank that was filled from an outside cistern by means of a force pump. Of even greater distinction was a lead bathtub.

Baking was done in a large brick oven in the kitchen, and three fireplaces did their best to heat at least a part of the lower floor. During recent alterations one of the original cranes was discovered while tearing out brickwork with which a fireplace had at some time been "modernized."

PLATE 122: *Courthouse at Hillsboro*

[201]

The seven or eight bedrooms were originally connected with the office and kitchen by means of wires, fastened to bells that hung on spiral springs; simple and admirable substitutes for house phones.

In the rear of the house is a stone smokehouse which is supposed to have been used also for the less savory purpose of storing furs for the trappers who stayed overnight at the tavern.

The great barn where horses were stabled and where the drivers doubtless slept when the tavern was overcrowded, is forty by fifty feet in size, and has remarkable framing of axe-hewn timbers.

COURTHOUSES

The early courthouses were inevitably classic in design. As temples of justice there was a natural tendency to revert to the Roman temple forms, even as the lawyers who functioned in them reverted to Roman codes. Moreover most of the older courthouses of the state were built when the classics were a veritable obsession in cultured circles, and Thomas Jefferson's Classic Revival was at its height. So we find some of the designs reminiscent of Jefferson's flair for things Roman, as for instance the Highland County courthouse (Plate 122) at Hillsboro, while others reflect the more sturdy structures of the Greeks, among these being the ones at Painesville in Lake County (Plate 123) and at Mount Vernon in Knox County (Plate 124). The courthouse at Mount Vernon has been somewhat "modernized" but nevertheless retains its classic dignity.

The fine old building at Painesville (that was built about 1840) has been superseded by a more pretentious neighbor, and now serves in an humbler capacity as city hall. But even that fate has been the means of preserving an excellent example of Greek Revival design. All too many of these old classic buildings have fallen before the onward march of that energetic but sadly misguided period that followed the Civil War.

COURTHOUSE, DAYTON

The courthouse at Dayton is an excellent example of the rein-

PLATE 123: *Old Lake County Courthouse, Painesville. Now used as a city hall. Built about 1838 to 1840*

[203]

PLATE 124: *Courthouse at Mount Vernon*

carnation of Greek temples into the life of our early nineteenth century. It expresses fully the spirit of classicism that led men's minds back to the realm of classic literature, dubbed countless cities of this country with classic names, and perpetuated Thomas Jefferson's obsession for classic architecture (Plate 125).

Local history and tradition tell us that inspiration for the design of this courthouse came from an engraving in a book which belonged to Horace Pease, a former citizen of Dayton. This engraving depicted the Theseum, best preserved of the temples at Athens, and was offered by Mr. Pease to the county commissioners as a design that possessed dignity and beauty suited to the proposed courthouse. Tentative floor plans and sketches were sent, with suggestions as to its classical prototype, to a Cincinnati architect named Howard Daniels, who prepared the necessary drawings and specifications. In so doing he made many changes, dropping the Doric order in favor of the Ionic, using columns to carry only the pediment, and substituting pilasters on the side walls for the columns of the original peripteral temple.

White limestone was used as a building material, producing a color effect well in accord with the style of architecture. The structure is entirely of masonry, the only wood being that in window sash, inner doors, and furniture.

A winding stairway of stone is carried to the second story, on the rear wall of the entrance lobby. This is self-sustaining, built on the cantilever principle, with the steps supported only where they rest against the wall. The central room, used as a probate court room, is elliptical in plan and is surmounted by a dome. It is fifty-two feet long by forty-two in width and the eye of the dome, through which the room is lighted, is forty-three feet above the floor. Work began on the building in 1848 and was completed in 1850. The cost was $100,000.00, a great sum of money in those days.

Political influences have attempted the destruction of this beautiful structure to make way for a modern office building, but fortunately wiser counsels have prevailed.

PLATE 125: *Courthouse at Dayton. Built in 1848-50*

Sandusky County Courthouse

At Fremont in Sandusky County is another of the fine examples of Classic Revival architecture that still remain as heritages from the early nineteenth century (Plate 126). It was built about 1840 to replace an earlier structure of frame. Records show that the county commissioners, at a meeting held June 2, 1840, opened proposals filed with them by various contractors, and awarded the contract for building the new courthouse to one Isaac Knapp, the consideration being $14,550.00. A further sum of $2,000.00 was later added to this amount.

The plans for the structure were drawn by a Mr. Williams, who placed in the basement a jail consisting of a series of dark and hopelessly safe dungeons. These may not conform to present-day ideals of prison housing, but they would certainly discourage enthusiasm for a criminal career on the part of anyone who had once been the recipient of this basement hospitality.

This courthouse has so much to commend it for preservation as a historic monument that, in spite of attempts to replace it with a modern building, the citizens of the county have consistently refused to sanction its destruction.

State House, Columbus

The design for Ohio's State House at Columbus, like that of the nation at Washington, was secured by means of a competition. In both the completed building embodies the ideas of several designers. The Ohio competition was inaugurated by an act of the Legislature which, on January 26, 1838, authorized the appointment of a commission to direct the erection of a State House to replace the inadequate structure then in use.

Three prizes were offered by the commission, the first of $500.00 being awarded to Henry Walter of Cincinnati; the second of $300.00 to Martin E. Thompson of New York City; and the third of $200.00 to Thomas Cole of Catskill, New York.

From these an acceptable design was worked out in which were

PLATE 126: *Courthouse at Fremont. Built about 1840*

embodied features from all three, and a contract was awarded to William S. Sullivant for limestone, at fifty cents per perch of twenty-five cubic feet, from his quarry on the Scioto River a few miles above the city. The labor was to be performed by convicts from the penitentiary.

The original estimate on the building was $450,000.00, but costs climbed in the manner customary with building operations until official records show that the completed structure involved an expenditure of $1,644,677.00.

Work began in the spring of 1839, and proceeded with such rapidity that the corner stone was laid, at the northeast angle of the building, on July 4th of the same year. Five or six thousand people attended the ceremony, which included music, a military parade, and what was most appreciated of all, presumably, a good dinner.

Satisfactory progress was made until agitation for the removal of the seat of government from Columbus caused the Legislature, on March 10, 1840, to repeal the act authorizing erection of the State House in spite of the fact that $40,000.00 had already been expended.

Operations ceased for nearly six years, but finally on February 21, 1846, a second act was passed which made it possible to resume operations. However, so small an appropriation was provided that but scant results were obtained, an average of barely seventeen convicts a day being maintained on the job throughout the year.

The public lost patience and the newspapers berated those in authority until at last a fresh start was made in the spring of 1848. About this time Henry Walter retired from business and William Russell West and J. O. Sawyer were appointed architects of the Capitol.

The basement walls were completed during the year, and in 1849 work was accelerated by the construction of a railroad to the quarry from which the stone was being taken. A liberal appropriation of funds also had a stimulating effect.

PLATE 127: *Façade of State House, Columbus. Built in 1839-1861*

The old State House burned quite providentially on February 1, 1852, rendering imperative the provision of quarters for the governmental departments.

Another architect, N. B. Kelly, was appointed in 1854, and in 1856 the plans were submitted to Thomas U. Walker of Washington and Richard Upjohn of New York, who had been retained as consulting architects. Few changes were made by them and the work was carried to completion without serious delay.

The building was opened formally on January 6, 1857, with another grand celebration, including of course the customary round of oratory, music, and food. On the following day the General Assembly met in its new quarters but construction work was not entirely completed until November, 1861.

Dimensions of the structure are three hundred and four feet long, by one hundred and eighty-four feet wide, with an area of slightly over two acres. Eight Doric columns, thirty-six feet high and six feet two inches in diameter, distinguish recessed porticos on the east and west fronts; the other two sides have similar features with four columns each. The heavy entablature is carried unbroken across the façades, supported by pilasters that continue the order of the central colonnades (Plate 127).

A dome, that was to have been the dominant feature of the building, had to be abandoned because of the public demand for economy, and in its place was built a circular drum that has been continuously maligned, and on occasion been dubbed with such painfully apt names as the "Chinese Hat" and the "Cheese Box." This unfortunate feature surmounts a central rotunda sixty-four feet, five inches in diameter, and one hundred and twenty feet in height from the marble floor to the eye of the dome.

PART VI

THE VERNACULAR

PLATE 128: *House near Seville. Note the "drawn out" Ionic capital that stretches across the doorway; also the use of converging flutes used apparently to exaggerate the entasis of the pilasters*

[214]

PART VI: THE VERNACULAR

ALONG with the fine craftsman-
ship that exists in so much of Ohio's early architecture are to be
found many examples of design in which the attempts of untrained
mechanics to interpret half-understood drawings verge closely on
the ludicrous or the pathetic. On the other hand these interpreta-
tions often command our admiration, revealing as they do rare ingenuity in solving problems of construction, and active imagination
in working out details of design with which the builders were unfamiliar.

Thus on the doorway at Streetsboro (Plate 31) and that of the
old dining hall at Hudson (Plate 53) the general form was derived undoubtedly from designs by the Brothers Adam of England,
or by Benjamin or Lafever of America. The small engravings in
the books on architecture showed little detail and were doubtless
puzzle pictures to many a builder who, nevertheless, went ahead
with the job of working out details that didn't mean a thing to him.
And so we find half-round turnings in place of flutings, many-
pointed stars and wooden rings instead of rosettes, and other strange
details in which imagination substituted for knowledge.

The clumsy attempts at classic pilasters, columns, mouldings,
and cornices often produced curious effects that would scarcely pass
muster in a school of architecture or a Beaux-Arts competition.
They were crude, the details often painfully misunderstood, yet
in them we recognize a sincerity that wins our admiration. Those
pioneer builders were creating a vernacular in architecture possessing
vitality and spontaneity that is often missing in highly sophisticated creations. We may smile at the clumsy results, but we must
admire the simple but direct thinking which they represent.

A most curious illustration of the naïve manner in which the

[215]

PLATE 129: *This doorway near North Bristol has the peculiar four-lobed rosette found on a mantel in Maine. Just what relation exists between these widely separated places someone else will have to determine*

[216]

builder blithely rang the changes on staid classic details is to be found on a doorway near Medina (Plate 128). The crude pilasters on either side are built with entasis, but, apparently feeling the need for more tapering lines to satisfy the eye, the builder deliberately ran flutings which converge from the base, toward the capital, thus solving, for his mind at least, the problem of giving entasis and lightness of proportion to the shaft.

But this genius did not stop there. He also introduced turned columns, with acorns at the top, on each side of the door and, surmounting each with one volute of an Ionic capital, he stretched that capital, in a triumphant flourish, completely across the doorway, making one capital to grow where two had always grown before.

To the purist it may seem merely funny, but I enjoy that doorway, for these crude attempts at interpreting the architectural forms of classic Greece and Rome reveal the gropings of an untutored mind toward things that are fine, and enable us to glimpse the struggles of our Ohio pioneers in establishing the foundations of the culture upon which their successors have built.

A most fascinating example of vernacular architectural detail, if I may be allowed to use the term, is found on a house (Plate 129) near North Bristol. Four pilasters stretch up the full two stories of the front, and at a distance give the effect of being delicately fluted. Closer examination (Plate 130) reveals not fluting, but shadows cast by successive ridges due to a curious form of laminated construction. Starting from the outer edges, the pilaster is built up of one-inch strips fastened side by side. Each strip is thrust outward from the wall, the projection decreasing toward the middle, until the two middle strips meet on the same plane. The effect, as seen from a little distance, is quite similar to fluting or reeding, and as the offsets grow successively less toward the middle, the shadows cast by them decrease, thus producing an optical illusion that exaggerates the apparent projection of the pilaster.

By a curious irony, the builder's imagination seems to have

PLATE 130: *Detail of pilaster, on house near North Bristol, showing ingenious use of laminated construction in creating effect of fluting or reeding*

PLATE 131: *House between Attica and Bellvue. An unusual example of the "Steamboat Gothic" type of architecture*

[219]

PLATE 132: *House at Old Washington. Note curious manner in which ends of stone courses are rounded on gable*

ceased to function at this point, and with a remarkable example of original construction to his credit, he gave up the struggle when he came to fit base and capital to his pilasters and, with sublime disregard for their semi-elliptical section, he calmly completed them with base and capital of rectangular plan.

Another builder got around the monotonous labor of planing reeds on mantel and chair rails, in the Farwell House at Hudson (Plate 172), by gluing short lengths of actual swamp reeds on the surface to be enriched, the projection of mouldings, top and bottom, effectually concealing the hollow structure of the reeds.

A most unusual gable treatment is seen on a stone house (Plate 132) in Old Washington, on the National Road. The walls were laid up beautifully with well-cut, dressed stone, and when the rake of the gable was reached, instead of finishing with a coping, with steps or with an overhanging cornice, this original genius terminated each course of stone with a complete half circle, stepping them back to follow the roof slant. One of the chimneys, which gave a finish at the ridge, had fallen when the accompanying photograph was taken, but has been rebuilt since, when the entire house was restored.

Two little houses at Palmyra (Plate 133) with the overly heavy entablature that was so common, quite emancipate themselves from mediocrity by their gable windows and front walls. The windows are naïvely "cut on the bias" to conform with the slant of the roof, thus affording a maximum of glass opening without cutting into the frieze. The builder didn't worry in the least about designing a window to fit the space; he just carried the top casing parallel with the roof, allowing it to cut as it would across the sash, which disappeared meekly behind the frieze.

He thought in terms of massiveness when he laid out the square pillars that carry the porch roof, and then achieved his masterpiece by paneling the wall beneath the porch with wainscoting that would have been a credit to the interior of a far more pretentious

PLATE 133: *House at Palmyra. The paneling under porch is a unique feature*

PLATE 134: *House at Zanesville. A good example of the so-called "Steamboat Gothic" type, with vertical siding and sawed-out tracery*

PLATE 135: *Cottage at Copley, with sawed-out lambrequin effect under eaves*

house. This cottage too would not qualify in a Beaux-Arts competition, but it has its points.

Then there is the jigsaw type of house that has drawn the lightning of ridicule and censure for lo, these many years. It had its fling when mining, inventing, promoting, and railroad building occupied the minds of able men, leaving the lesser ones to cultivate the arts; when S. F. B. Morse quit painting portraits to invent the telegraph, and Jephthah H. Wade laid aside his camera to organize the Western Union Telegraph Company.

Little minds are prone to attempt "something different," and as the time was about ripe for a change in architectural style, the carpenter-architects threw away their Palladois, Benjamins, and Lafevers and placed their faith in jigsaws.

They became enamored of the possibilities for reproducing Gothic masonry by means of pine boards, a hangover probably from Horace Walpole's earlier experiments at Strawberry Hill. This Gothic epidemic was widespread and, because of its apt use of pseudo-Gothic details as ornament on Mississippi steamboats, has been dubbed "Steamboat Gothic."

The most amazing battlements, tracery, oriel windows, arched windows, and doorways, as well as other medieval details were created by the coördination of boards and jigsaws. Other styles of architecture also were sacrificed on the altar of this strange architectural cult, which for some reason, unknown to modern man, was dubbed Queen Anne.

Houses of this type are universally acknowledged to be bad, yet on several occasions when I have photographed them for use as "horrible examples," that purpose was abandoned, for the photographs didn't qualify with quite the necessary degree of badness. One of these is shown on Plate 134. The little portico on Plate 131 seems to meet the specifications for undesirable qualities, yet I find myself becoming quite fascinated with the curlycues over the entrance and the prim little frets on either side. As for the little cottage at Copley (Plate 135), I have lost my heart quite unreservedly to the jigsawed valance under the eaves. The fascination of those festoons and drops is not to be denied. Then see the way in which the Greek wave ornament has carried those festoons up the slant of the roof!

This chapter is not for the purist, and although it might be continued indefinitely with endless examples for illustration, I fear that my reputation may demand that it be closed. In self-defense I must recall the facts that Greek builders carved marble skulls of oxen on their temple friezes; transmuted timber construction into marble; and compelled marble maidens to support heavy entablatures on their heads; so maybe our poor Victorian carpenters may be forgiven their trespasses in the realm of wooden masonry.

PART VII
CONSTRUCTION AND DETAILS

PLATE 136: *Log house near Sinking Spring*

PART VII: CONSTRUCTION AND DETAILS

THE earliest houses erected by Ohio's pioneers were to a large extent built of logs (Plate 136) laid horizontally, notched together at the corners, and chinked with mud to close the crevices. Contrary to general belief, these snug cabins were not the type that was built by the Pilgrims and Puritans of the Massachusetts Bay neighborhood. They built dugouts in side hills or crude huts with walls of wattle, or of palings set upright in the ground.

It remained for the Swedes and Finns who settled in the Delaware Valley about 1638, to introduce the use of horizontal logs in building walls. They came from a land where timber was plentiful, which was not the case in England where stone and brick were the building materials in common use.

The log cabin of the Swedes was an excellent protection against both cold and heat, but the Anglo-Saxon instinct for comfortable home life was too strong to be satisfied long with dwellings of so crude a character and, having won the first struggle over nature, the Ohio immigrants began to build homes that recalled those they had left behind in the east. These were largely adaptations from the English Georgian style, or followed the prevailing mode of the Classic Revival; but whatever might be the style, the material used was largely timber. To be sure brick was used to a considerable extent, especially in the southern part of the state where the southern traditions prevailed, and some use was made of stone, but with the vast forests not only available for use but standing in the way of necessary cultivation of the soil, timber was the logical material for building.

Labor, not materials, was the item to be conserved, and as there were few sawmills to cut up the logs, it was necessary to hew them

PLATE 137: *Framework of old house at Coddingville. Probably built by man named Codding, who came from Canandaigua County, New York*

to shape by hand. Thus heavy timbers were the most economical and the buildings were framed with vast adze-hewn beams instead of the light balloon construction of today. Heavy timbers meant fewer of them, hence additional economy of labor. They also meant more durable buildings. Nails and bolts had to be forged by hand, so we find that wooden pegs were used largely in fastening the timbers together.

Masterly skill was shown in planning the framework of these old buildings, involving an expert knowledge of stresses and strains, especially in working out roof trusses and some of the more pretentious church steeples. It is only fair to say that much valuable aid was had in this connection from the books published by Asher Benjamin and his contemporaries. The most elaborate instructions are given for framing, for laying out stairways, and building roof trusses as well as for working out such details as cornices and Ionic capitals.

The manner of framing is shown to excellent advantage in Plates 137 and 138, which show an old house that had literally been reduced to a skeleton. Framing that shows great knowledge of timber construction is found also in many of the old covered bridges (Plate 139).

The "raising" of these frames was observed as a community holiday. The men volunteered their services in handling the heavy timbers, and the women prepared incredible amounts of food to sustain the muscles and nerves in this "ticklish" as well as ponderous undertaking. It was "ticklish" too, for unless every movement of every man was under perfect direction and control, a timber might slip, and such a slip was quite apt to mean serious injury or death to luckless workers.

The timbers were all hewn and shaped preparatory to the raising, and a glance at the skeleton building will suggest the hazard involved in lifting the heavy beams into position, and holding them poised while the pins were hammered into place. This was before the day of donkey engines, motors, and hoists. A keg of whiskey was an almost inseparable adjunct of the "house raisings" and prodigies of strength were achieved under its spell.

Where lumber was to be sawn a "saw pit" was provided, before the day of power-driven mills. With one man above and another in the pit, the saw bit its way through the log with surprising rapidity. Plaster, in the earlier work, was usually laid over split lath; that is, thin boards split irregularly lengthwise of the grain so they might be spread open, something like a crude mesh, on the same principle that is now applied to expanded metal lath. Shingles were split, and all finish was made by hand, including surfacing and moulding.

Each joiner had his own moulding planes with which he ran his mouldings, and to their credit it may be said that their mouldings were usually very beautiful in section. They had never gotten the knack of making ugly things, an art in which their descendants excelled.

It is said that in running long heavy mouldings, and the flutings of large columns, a horse was sometimes hitched to the plane, drawing it the length of the timber and leaving to the carpenter only the delicate task of guiding the knife.

The earlier mouldings, of interiors especially, had a delicacy of scale that is found in eighteenth and early nineteenth century work of the eastern states; a refinement that is essentially in key with material as fine grained and workable as the pine and other woods that were used here commonly for interior trim. The later work shows equal refinement, but a larger scale, due doubtless to the fact that details of the nineteenth century Classic Revival were taken from Palladio's plates and from other similar works, which reproduced details designed originally for marble and stone, materials which naturally called for larger scale and fewer members.

This tendency may be traced back to Thomas Jefferson, who, in working out details for his classic buildings, followed precedent

PLATE 138: *Framework of old house at Coddingville, Granger Township. Note details of framing shown here and on Plate 137*

[233]

PLATE 139: *Covered bridge near Jacksonville*

[234]

meticulously and took literally from Palladio's plates details for his interior woodwork, regardless of the material for which they were originally designed. This resulted in a dignified simplicity that is quite in contrast with the feminine delicacy of earlier work that may be traced back to the Brothers Adam of England.

DOORS AND WINDOWS

Upon the doorway was lavished the utmost of loving care by the builders. Here they displayed their skill in design and construction; here they showed what they were capable of doing, and suggested what they might have done but for the handicap of restricted means. The rest of the house might be plain to asceticism, but here the almost pathetic desire for beauty was allowed some opportunity for gratification (Plates 144-150).

The variety of designs found on the doorways of our simple farmhouses is amazing, and suggests the architectural wealth that might have been ours but for the restraint imposed upon our early craftsmen by the rigid limitations of pioneer pocketbooks. Endless changes were rung upon the limited forms of these old structures in spite of the meager resources of the builders, and seldom are two doorways found to be exactly alike. Yet the inspiration for all was drawn from Georgian and Neo-Classic sources. Study of the photographs reproduced throughout this book will make this more evident than will any amount of explanation.

Windows were usually very plain, with double-hung sash divided into small panes, and enclosed within a simple frame. Occasionally we find that mouldings were added, and more rarely a bit of detail, carved or otherwise, gave a touch of elegance. Usually, however, the green shutters, which were an almost universal adjunct, gave all the accent that was deemed necessary to dignify the scheme of fenestration.

FAN LIGHTS

Although the doorway was the architectural feature that most frequently tempted the Ohio builder from the paths of Puritanical

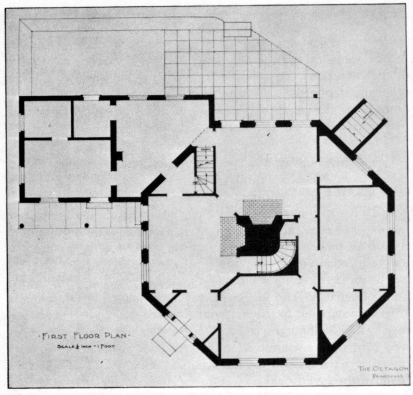

·FIRST FLOOR PLAN·

SCALE ⅛ INCH = 1 FOOT

THE OCTAGON
PAINESVILLE

PLATE 140: *Octagon House, Painesville—First floor plan. (Drawings re-produced through courtesy of Francis R. Bacon, Dean of The School of Architecture, Western Reserve University.)*

plainness, the gable fan light was equally alluring. Here too he could indulge in a bit of playfulness, provide needed light or ventilation in the attic, and add immeasurably to the charm of his house. So we often find most delightful bits of detail tucked away up in the gable beneath the overhanging cornice. Sometimes there is only a semi-elliptical sash in which the glass is divided into fanciful patterns by leads or wood muntins; again a delicate fan-shaped louver which conceals the glass is enclosed by a more or less ornate frame; occasionally the fan is merely a bit of applied ornament designed to enrich the otherwise uninteresting gable (Plates 151-160).

FAÇADES

Façades of the more pretentious houses were often given an architectural treatment involving the use of a classic order. This may take the form of pilasters in low relief and other details of similar delicacy, as on the Baldwin-Buss House at Hudson (Plate 56), or it may degenerate into a crude and clumsy imitation of the order. Yet, strangely enough, in spite of clumsy proportions and impossible details, the work of these pioneer carpenters was surprisingly good. Even the worst of the pseudo-classical buildings possessed a simple dignity that maintained them at an artistic level far above that of the succeeding jigsaw and turning-lathe era.

On gable ends the entablature was sometimes carried entirely across, completely enclosing the triangular pediment (Plates 36, 56, 97, and 98); in others it continued only the width of a pilaster, which often did not exist, and there stopped, with the mouldings returning upon themselves (Plates 19 and 89).

Sometimes four pilasters carry the entablature (Plates 36, 56, and 97), but more often there is but one on each side (Plate 19). In the former type a very flat arch sometimes cuts into the architrave or frieze (Plate 97), a feature that is quite common in western New York State.

Brick houses were frequently built with hip roofs (Plate 99),

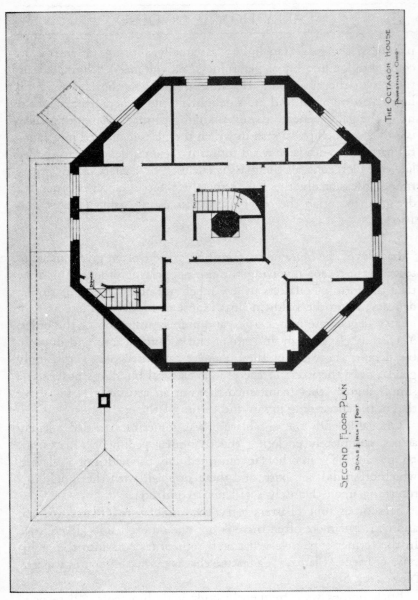

SECOND FLOOR PLAN
SCALE ⅛ INCH = 1 FOOT

THE OCTAGON HOUSE
PAINESVILLE · OHIO

PLATE 141: *Octagon House—Second floor plan*

and more rarely with pitched roofs terminating against stepped gables at the ends (Plate 101). Still more unusual was the gambrel roof (Plate 50), which was so common in Connecticut that it seems strange the fashion was not followed more commonly in Ohio, especially in the Western Reserve. A rare treatment of the crowning members of a wall is found on the house shown in Plate 107. Four corbeled courses of bricks, with headers set diagonally, form a cornice that follows the rake of the gable and is also carried across the front. At the corners a stone block is cut to receive the projecting courses of brick.

Public buildings and the better class of dwellings were often enriched with classic ornament such as the dentil (Plates 43 and 164), the modillion (Plates 57 and 98), and other details of Greek and Roman origin (Plates 11, 43, 164 and 165).

GRILLES AND FRETS

Akin to fan lights in function were the grilles and frets that were sometimes inserted in the frieze as a means of lighting and ventilating attic rooms. These too were sometimes used merely for decorative effect (Plate 165), and although usually sawed from wood, the grilles were occasionally cast in iron and the one just referred to was cut in stone. The decorative note thus added was often the dominant feature of the design (Plates 161 to 166).

INTERIOR TRIM

An infinite variety of treatment was given the interior trim. It was seldom ornate, nor did it often include wall paneling, other than that below the chair rail. Wainscoted walls had gone out of fashion before settlers invaded the Ohio Country, and as lime was available for making plaster, the builders were not forced to sheath their rooms with boards as were the early settlers of New England. This was done, rather crudely, in rare instances, but the general custom was to follow the late eighteenth-century fashion and use only a low dado, occasionally, however, paneling the fireplace end of the room.

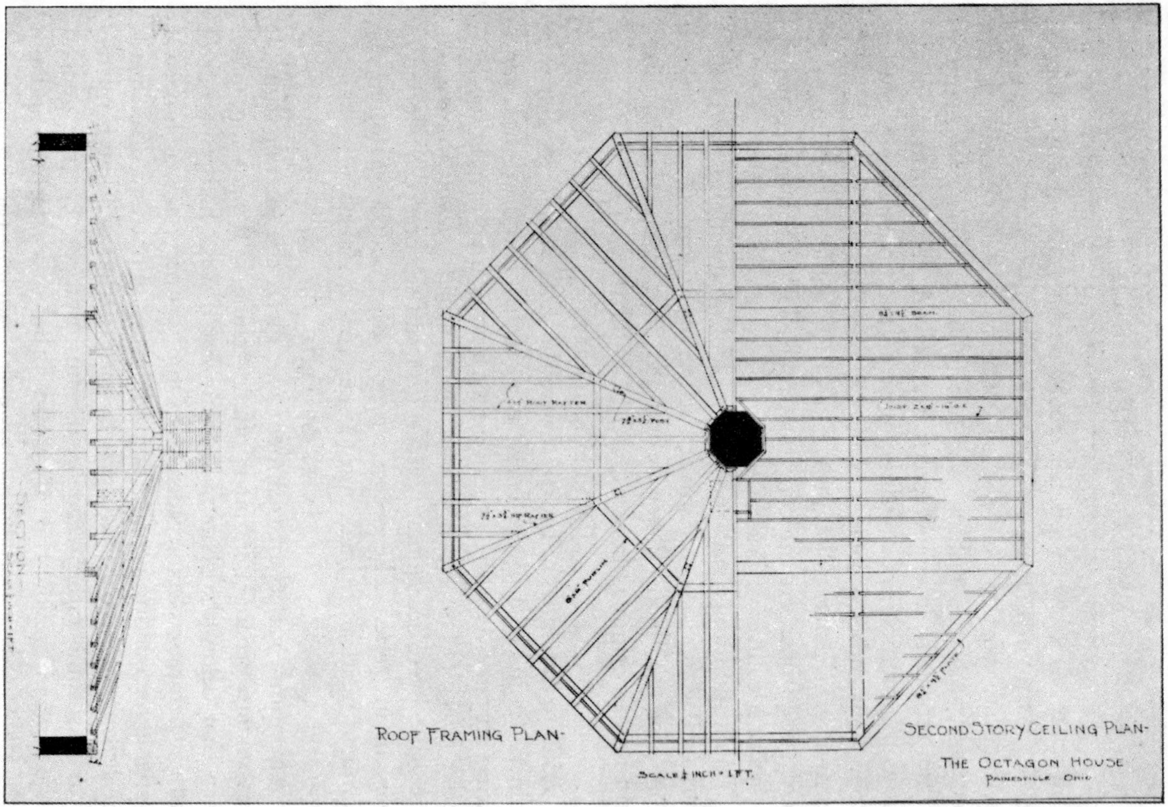

SECOND STORY CEILING PLAN·

THE OCTAGON HOUSE
Painesville Ohio

ROOF FRAMING PLAN·

SCALE⅛ INCH=1FT·

SECTION·
Scale ⅛ inch = 1 Ft·

PLATE 142: *Octagon House—Framing plan*

EARLY HOMES OF OHIO

Rich detail, such as distinguishes the great mansions of the Atlantic seaboard, was beyond the means of pioneers west of the Alleghenies, and it is rarely indeed that we find woodwork as well executed and rich in detail as the mantel at Mount Oval (Plate 25). Life was simple in the Ohio Country during the first half century after its settlement by white men, and architectural luxury went little further than well-executed paneling, with occasionally some simple carving or a job of ornamental plaster.

As doorways were the exterior features chosen for embellishment, so the mantel was in the interior. It was the source of warmth and good cheer for the family, and the builders quite naturally lavished upon it their greatest care.

The earlier house had a large fireplace for cooking, with a swinging crane to hold the kettles. Built into the chimney, and sometimes slightly removed from the fireplace, was the bake oven which was often concealed when not in use by a hinged wainscot panel. The oven was placed at a convenient height from the floor, with a chamber underneath which may have been used for storage. It was heated by building a fire within it, or by shoveling into it hot embers from the fireplace. When the walls were sufficiently heated the coals were raked out, the things to be baked were placed inside, the opening closed, and the oven left to perform its allotted function.

The skill displayed by our grandmothers of the north, and the colored "mammies" of the south, in preparing elaborate feasts with these crude fireplaces and ovens, puts to shame the present-day cook with her scientifically-constructed devices that act automatically with the turn of a gas valve or the pressure of an electric button.

Other rooms were heated by fireplaces of varying sizes and degrees of ornamental effect. The facing was usually of red brick with a hearth of brick or perhaps of stone. Toward the middle of the century cast-iron facings were often used, the designs of which were sometimes of surprising beauty, and indicative of great skill

[241]

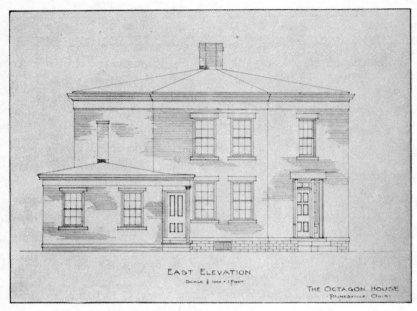

PLATE 143: *Octagon House—East elevation*

on the part of the pattern makers and the iron founders by whom they were made (Plate 16).

Regardless of the romance that clusters about the fireside, and the charm which it adds to the room, it was a wasteful and laborious way of heating. With the invention of the Franklin stove many of the fireplaces were bricked up and the more efficient cast-iron heater was installed in front, with only a small smoke pipe connected with the chimney to carry off the smoke and create the draft necessary for combustion (Plate 14).

The early Ohio builders usually designed their mantels in conformity with the traditions of the late eighteenth or early nineteenth century, usually the latter. The mantels seldom formed part of a paneled wall, as had been an earlier custom in the east, though flanking doors and cupboards sometimes combined to produce that effect. The classic order was the usual basis of design, with a column or pilaster on each side supporting an entablature, but with details that were often less reminiscent of the Greeks and Romans than of the country carpenter's fancy; yet they were usually dignified and frequently possessed of real distinction, as may be seen by referring to Plates 24 and 25, and 167 to 172 inclusive.

Considerable fertility of invention was displayed both in the general forms and in the details. Pilasters were either plain (Plates 16 and 168), paneled, or moulded (Plate 14) like the door architraves of Asher Benjamin. Columns were plain, fluted or reeded, the latter treatment being seen on the twin colonnettes in Plates 171 and 172.

The common practice was followed of breaking the frieze with a projection in the middle and over the columns or pilasters (Plates 25, 170, 171 and 172), but in many instances the frieze was carried unbroken the full width of the mantel. Decorative details were often crudely drawn and executed, as for instance the curiously inaccurate attempts at ellipses on Plates 171 and 172. On the other hand examples of carving are to be found that show a high degree of skill, as in the rosettes on Plates 180 and 184.

The use of ormolu rosettes on French Empire woodwork and furniture is reflected in the carved ornament seen in Plate 168, and an original, if not highly successful effect has been achieved on the mantel in Plate 167 by the use on the frieze of a moulding similar to those on door frames, and the substitution of a crude fret for the architrave moulding.

Mouldings range from the elaborate and wholly unclassical profiles of Plate 25 to the practical elimination of such embellishment in Plate 168. The heavy members and austere restraint displayed in such designs is an evident throwback to the First Empire.

Thus in the later work is seen the influence of Percier and Fontaine of Napoleon's realm and of Thomas Jefferson in our own. The earlier and more delicate designs with their reeded columns, sunbursts, and flutings reflect the style of the Brothers Adam in England, and their American followers Bulfinch and McIntire.

INTERIOR DOORWAYS

Interior doors, like those on the exteriors, vary in the arrangement and number of panels, and in the profile of mouldings that enclose them. Reference to the plates will be more illuminating than a lengthy dissertation on the subject.

The casings also display much ingenuity in the development of varied effects. Some are merely flat boards which stop against plinths and corner blocks, and are perhaps simply ornamented as shown in Plate 173 or less usually with a crowning feature as in Plate 174. Most common are the moulded architraves, such as are found in considerable variety in the works of Asher Benjamin (Plate 181), which stop against more or less ornate plinth and corner blocks. Some of these make effective use of fluting, reeding, and various forms of mouldings, often deeply undercut.

STAIRWAYS

Stairways are often of surprisingly good design, the ends of the

PLATE 144: *Peck House, Portsmouth*

[245]

PLATE 145: *Doorway of church at Zoar. Built in 1853*

steps being enriched with applied scrolls and the handrails simply but delicately worked out in walnut with balusters of the same wood. The balusters are sometimes turned, but more often are rectangular in section, and are set with the narrow edge to the end of the step, thus giving a pleasing effect of delicacy.

The richly-carved stairways of the seaboard are practically unknown in early Ohio houses. The hardy pioneers had neither time nor wealth to provide such luxuries, yet the craftsmanship displayed in the woodwork of their homes is of a character that is to be found in only the finest construction today. This craftsmanship is seen at its best in some of the finer stairways, with handrails that sweep into a spiral on the bottom step in lieu of a newel post, and in some instances are carried in unbroken curves up through three stories. Here again the builders were indebted to the ever-helpful Asher Benjamin, whose books contain minute instructions and exact drawings that made plain the intricate details of stair building. An excellent example of the stair builder's art is found in the Curtis-Devin House at Mount Vernon (Plates 104 and 105. Also Plates 182-183).

THE OCTAGONAL PLAN

The curious arrangements of rooms evolved by those who have followed Thomas Jefferson's fancy for compressing a house plan into an octagon have already been mentioned (Page 47). The house near Painesville is an excellent example of the octagonal type, which is found in comparatively small numbers as compared with the temple form of classic building, that we owe also to Jefferson.

The writer on octagonal houses, previously quoted on Page 51, parades a convincing array of figures that prove beyond any possibility of argument that mankind has shown unmitigated stupidity throughout the ages by insisting upon rectangular houses, and houses with wings, instead of going in for octagons. He clinches the matter by the final argument that thin animals and people (animals come first), are less comely than "fleshy" ones, because they tend to the angular rather than to the spherical. This principle is applied also to the relative beauties of chestnut burrs versus apples and peaches. The obvious deduction is that "a square house is more beautiful than a triangular one, and an octagon or duodecagon than either."

Plans for house, barn, schoolhouse, and church prove the practical superiority of the octagon over the rectangle as a basis of plan, and leave the house with projecting wings entirely without excuse for being. The latter is completely devastated by a sally into the realm of humor, in which the author slily observes that "Wings on houses are not in quite as good taste as on birds. Well! The argument is irrefutable—the octagon wins.

The drawings of the Painesville house (Plates 140, 141, 142, and 143) show a practical working out of the octagonal problem, in a way that has produced a most livable and convenient home.

THE GARFIELD-ROOT HOUSE, SHEFFIELD

An unusual built-in feature is to be found in the kitchen-dining room of the Garfield-Root House, near Sheffield in Lorain County. Between two doors was built a niche, fitted to receive a clock which has occupied this place of vantage since the house was finished. Below the shelf on which the clock stands are four small drawers, the whole forming a useful as well as original feature of the room.

A large fireplace distinguishes the opposite side of the room, and in the outside wall beside a door that opens on the back porch is a small, shallow cupboard designed as a convenient place to keep the ever necessary rifle of the pioneer. It was found, however, that the firearms rusted in this exposed position behind the clapboards and its use, for that purpose, was abandoned.

The house was built in 1839 for Milton Garfield by two carpenters from Avon, Ezra and Roswell Jackson. The interior of the main portion of the house was the work of Henry and Halsey Garfield, while the dining room is supposed to have been done by the Jacksons (Plate 185).

PLATE 146: *Elijah Pickering House, St. Clairsville*

PLATE 147: *Swift House, formerly in Swift's Hollow, near Vermillion. Burned in 1923*

PLATE 148: *Renick House, near Circleville. Erected in 1832. This door opens from a recessed side porch into a bedroom that has no communication with the other rooms of the house; it having been planned for the use of herdsmen. Note the paneled ceiling*

[251]

PLATE 149: *Doorway with inlaid pilasters*

[252]

PLATE 150: *Kinsman House, Kinsman*

PLATE 151: *Fan light, Hudson*

PLATE 152: *Fan light, Hudson*

PLATE 153: *Fan light, old dining hall, Western Reserve College, Hudson*

PLATE 154: *Fan light, Twinsburg*

PLATE 155: *Fan light, Marietta*

PLATE 156: *Fan light, Gates House, Gates Mills. Burned in 1935*

PLATE 157: *Fan light, Sunbury Tavern, Sunbury*

PLATE 158: *Fan light, Hudson*

[257]

PLATE 159: *Fan light*

PLATE 160: *Fan light, Mathews House, Painesville*

PLATE 161: *Frets—Top, on Lebanon Pike near Sharonville; bottom, near Shalersville*

PLATE 162: *Frets—Top, near Wellington; bottom, Circleville*

PLATE 163: *Frets—Top, near Bellvue; bottom, Huntington*

[261]

PLATE 164: *Fret, Lebanon*

PLATE 165: *Fret, Wooster*

[263]

PLATE 166: *Frets—Top, Bishop McIlvaine House, Gambier; bottom, Goldsmith Cottage, Painesville*

[264]

PLATE 167: *Mantel in Red Brick Tavern, Lafayette. Built in 1837*

PLATE 168: *Mantel in Seymour House, Hudson*

PLATE 169: *Mantel in Headquarters Building, Camp Sherman, Chillicothe*

[267]

PLATE 170: *Mantel in Headquarters Building, Camp Sherman*

[268]

PLATE 171: *Mantel in Headquarters Building, Camp Sherman*

[269]

PLATE 172: *Parlor mantel in Farwell House, Hudson*

PLATE 173: *Hall doorway, Avery-Downer House, Granville*

[271]

PLATE 174: *Hall Doorway, Effinger House, Lancaster*

PLATE 175: *Hall in Adams-Gray House, Adams Mills*

[273]

PLATE 176: *Interior trim of house near Lancaster*

PLATE 177: *Doorway, Smith House, Adams Mills*

PLATE 178: *Living room, Renick-Young House, near Circleville*

PLATE 179: *Buckingham House, Zanesville*

PLATE 180: *Curved doorway in Bate-Brinkerhoff House, Melmore*

PLATE 181: *Sections of architraves (door and window casings). Plate XLVII, in Asher Benjamin's "The Architect, or Practical House Carpenter," edition of 1848*

PLATE 182: *Stairway in McNeill House, near Waverly*

[280]

PLATE 183: *Stairway in Adams-Gray House, Adams Mills*

PLATE 184: *Window in Mathews House, Painesville*

[282]

PLATE 185: *Dining room of Milton Garfield House, Sheffield. Built in 1839. The alcove between the doors was built to receive the clock*

[283]

PART VIII

FOUR HISTORIC TOWNS

PLATE 186: *Law office of Elisha Whittlesey, Canfield*

PART VIII: FOUR HISTORIC TOWNS

I ndividual structures, successful builders, and distinctive details have occupied our attention to a great extent thus far. Now it may not be amiss to direct our attention to the historic and architectural features of certain selected towns. A group of four has been chosen because of peculiar relationships existing between them geographically, or through the association of prominent personalities with their early history.

All four of these towns are located in northern Ohio; two in the eastern portion of the Western Reserve; the others in that territory west of the Reserve known as the Firelands. Three are county seats, hence are inevitably associated with members of the legal profession; the fourth is famous chiefly as the birthplace of one of the world's greatest scientific inventors.

This group might be expanded indefinitely, for Ohio possesses innumerable towns fully as historic as the four chosen, and with old houses as interesting architecturally or because of traditions and associations. However, these seem sufficient for the purpose, and are presented merely as being typical and as possible lure to those who may be tempted to search out for themselves other places equally worthy of discovery.

Canfield

Many of the small towns possess backgrounds of history that add to their old houses a glamour in excess of their intrinsic architectural worth. Distinguished occupants have bequeathed to them a rich legacy of sentimental associations. An example of this is found in the old town of Canfield. Here a tiny brick building (Plate 186) facing the spacious village green has long stood empty, with its shutters closed. Yet for many years, in the early part of the last century, it was the busy law office of one of Ohio's most dis-

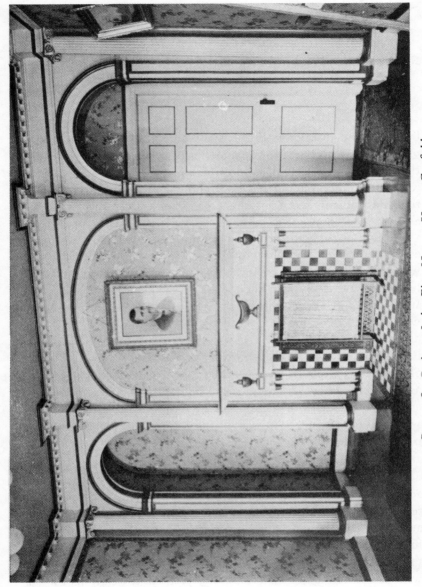

PLATE 187: *Parlor in Judge Eben Newton House, Canfield*

tinguished citizens, Elisha Whittlesey (born 1783, died 1863).

He came to Ohio in 1807 from Connecticut. His inventory of worldly possessions was unpleasantly close to nothing, but he was accompanied by a devoted wife, and had within himself courage, ability, and uprightness of character that made possible a notable career. He was successively a brigade major, an aide, and private secretary to General Harrison during the War of 1812; a member of the Ohio Legislature for two years; a member of Congress fifteen years (1822-1837); a founder of the Whig party; Auditor of the United States Treasury for the Postoffice Department; and first Comptroller of the Treasury. This office was held by him under four administrations, the last being Lincoln's. He was also general agent of the Washington Monument Association.

The little brick building at Canfield was Whittlesey's office, and here some of Ohio's most brilliant lawyers spent their student days. Among them was Joshua R. Giddings, who walked forty miles from his home in Jefferson to Canfield that he might study under this distinguished man. He had made no previous arrangement, had practically no money, but was received cordially, and by miraculous economy and hard work managed to sustain himself until he was admitted to the bar. He later became a most successful lawyer and a spectacular member of Congress.

The old Whittlesey homestead is on a rise of ground west of the village green, and is one of the oldest houses in Canfield. The roof cornice has the delicate mouldings, found in Colonial work, that distinguish the older houses from those of the later Classic Revival. One of the members is enriched by delicate beading.

The mantels are simple in form and detail, having a moulding or architrave around the facing, and a shelf supported by projecting mouldings. A bake oven, concealed by a door, is built into the chimney beside the kitchen fireplace. This oven is unusually large and is arched from front to back as well as from side to side. The great chimney is carried on three sustaining brick arches in the cellar.

PLATE 188: *Detail of Courthouse, Canfield*
[290]

Close by and facing the north end of the green is the former home of Judge Eben Newton who, in 1822, formed a law partnership with Elisha Whittlesey that lasted until Whittlesey's appointment by President Harrison as Auditor of the Treasury.

This house has an entablature of excellent detail, and an enormous oval sunburst in the pediment, similar to that on the Kennan House at Norwalk (Plate 190). The distinguishing feature here is the parlor trim. Attenuated Ionic columns in all four corners carry returns of the entablature, and on the mantel wall four columns give accent to a series of three arches. In the middle is the mantel; the other two arches frame alcoves, the depth of the chimney return, one of which serves as a passageway to an adjoining room (Plate 187).

The mantel entablature is supported by twin colonnettes at each side, and on the frieze are carved crude adaptations of Adam urns. The carving, together with mouldings and the modillions of the room cornice, have all been accented by the use of gilding, an embellishment of doubtful esthetic value that has been added in recent years.

At the opposite end of the village green stands the courthouse, begun in 1842 when the town of Canfield was made the seat of Mahoning County and used until 1879 when Youngstown wrested that honor from her smaller neighbor. The old building is of brick, with walls strengthened by pilasters which carry an excellent Doric entablature (Plate 188), that suggests the same classic origin as does the Matthews portico at Zanesville (Plates 11 and 76).

Numerous houses in and about Canfield are deserving of recognition, but few if any have the tradition of personalities connected with them that is associated with the Whittlesey House.

NORWALK

The story of Norwalk in a way continues that of Canfield, for the name of Elisha Whittlesey is closely associated with both. He came in 1815 with another lawyer, Platt Benedict, to attend the

PLATE 189: *Wooster-Boalt House, Norwalk. Built about 1848 as a Presbyterian school for girls*

Huron County Court at a town called Avery, in Milan township, which has long since disappeared. Both men were impressed with the possibilities of a near-by tract of high land known as Sandy Ridge for development as a town site and, after taking a third man, Frederic Fallig, into their confidence they made plans to relocate the county seat on the ridge.

Benedict rode on horseback to Connecticut where he purchased the land for about $2.15 per acre. Legislation was secured authorizing the appointment of a commission to locate a county seat, and the trio of promoters secured a decision in favor of Sandy Ridge, Whittlesey giving his personal bond for damages that might be claimed by the property owners of Avery.

The first actual settler of the new town was Platt Benedict, who arrived in 1817 and named the place Norwalk, probably after Norwalk, Connecticut. This was one of the towns whose burning by the British, during the Revolutionary War, led to the establishment of the Firelands as a means of reimbursing those whose property had been destroyed under similar circumstances. Benedict, who was born in 1775, was a child of four when the British burned Norwalk while on their way to his own home town of Danbury.

Whittlesey did not make his home in Norwalk, but nevertheless he left an indelible impress upon it. He suggested the planting of shade trees along both sides of the main street, a feature that still gives distinction to the place, and in various other ways he contributed to the town's upbuilding.

Norwalk was long famous as an educational center, and one of the early schools was housed in a three-story brick building erected for the purpose by Whittlesey. Among the men who were enrolled in one or another of the Norwalk schools were Rutherford B. Hayes; Charles Foster, afterward Governor of Ohio; and General McPherson, who took a distinguished part in the Civil War and was also a United States Senator. Among the schools for girls was one conducted by the Presbyterians who erected, about 1848, a brick

PLATE 190: *Sturgis-Kennan-Fulstow House, Norwalk. Built before 1835*

building that was purchased in 1858 by H. M. Wooster and converted into a private residence (Plate 189). Through the marriage of his daughter the house passed into the Boalt family, and her descendants still occupy the place.

Not far from this house, on the opposite side of the main street, is the Sturgis-Kennan-Fulstow House (Plate 190), which was built about 1834 by Thaddeus Sturgis. It was sold by Sturgis to Jairus Kennan, an uncle of George Kennan, the explorer and writer, whose exposure of conditions in Siberia under the Czarist régime, through articles published in the *Century Magazine,* shocked the world and won wide fame for the author. The Sturgis-Kennan-Fulstow House has a Classic Revival front with a pediment supported by four octagonal columns. On this pediment is a huge, oval sunburst which is strikingly like the one on the Newton House at Canfield. This house was either designed and built by William Gale Meade or was remodeled by him. Another house by this same builder is the Vredenburgh-Gardiner House. This was built about 1830 for John Vredenburgh and was sold to the Gardiner family who have added extensively to the original house, and in whose possession it still remains. Meade was the grandfather of Frank B. Meade, well-known architect of Cleveland.

Another of Norwalk's fine old homes is the Kimball-Wooster-Martin House (Plates 191 and 192), which was built for Moses Kimball in 1831. It was sold to Nathaniel Wooster about 1841 and is still occupied by his descendants.

According to family tradition the plan duplicates an ancestral home of the Kimballs in England. The original window glass is supposed to have been shipped from England, and the same origin is assigned to the brick of which it is built. The legend of imported English brick is frequently encountered in connection with old houses along the Atlantic coast, but rarely so far inland. It is a persistent, though seldom authenticated tradition regarding which Fiske Kimball writes in his *American Domestic Architecture,*

PLATE 191: *Kimball-Wooster-Martin House, Norwalk*

EARLY HOMES OF OHIO

"Contradicting the oft-repeated assertion about old houses, that the bricks were brought from England or from Holland, is the universal consensus of students of the records that importation of brick in the English colonies was negligible where it was not completely unknown. In general, the traditional statements regarding brick from England or Holland seem to rest initially on popular misinterpretation of the phrases English and Flemish bond." The terms English and Flemish bond refer to the manner in which the bricks were laid up in the wall.

Brick was burned quite commonly throughout the country, even in early Colonial times, and as clay and fuel were plentiful the cost of brick, even in Colonial Virginia, was lower than in England, making it quite improbable that brick would be brought across the Atlantic in any considerable quantity. It is peculiarly interesting to find this tradition in what was, at the time the house in question was built, the far western frontier, for difficulties of transportation by canal, lake, and overland would have rendered the cost practically prohibitive.

Glass, being lighter and less bulky, was more generally imported though there were glass factories in the new world from the time of the Jamestown settlement, and Ohio itself had a glass factory at Zanesville as early as 1815.

The fine houses of Norwalk, as in many other Ohio towns, were being built at the very time when the Jeffersonian tradition was supplanting the Colonial and Georgian. These houses date from the '30s and '40s when the architectural publications of Asher Benjamin and Minard Lafever were spreading broadcast their designs in the Roman and Greek manner. Builders were doubtless eager to prove themselves abreast of the latest fashions and their clients equally desirous of showing their progressiveness in keeping up to these fashions by building in the latest mode. So we find in this group of Norwalk houses, all built within a decade or so, that the eighteenth-century spirit was giving way to that of the nine-

PLATE 192: *Kimball-Wooster-Martin House, Norwalk*

[298]

teenth, and the classicism of Georgian England was being supplanted by the classicism of Rome and Greece. This change is made strikingly evident by comparing the Kimball-Wooster-Martin with the Wooster-Boalt or Sturgis-Kennan-Fulstow Houses.

MILAN

The claim of Milan to a place in this particular quartette of Ohio towns is based chiefly on its proximity to Norwalk. Not that it has no claims of its own to greatness, for it has, in fact it was once a prosperous shipbuilding town, and was reputed in its day to have been one of the largest grain shipping ports in the world, a claim that is inconceivable today when scarcely a trace is to be seen of the canal which carried the ships down the valley to Lake Erie, or of the warehouses into which poured the flood of grain from this part of the Ohio Country.

Then too, Milan may well demand a share of glory from her larger neighbor, for it will be remembered that from Milan Township Norwalk filched the county seat for her own.

With its commercial and political supremacy gone, Milan still possesses the dignified charm that is the legacy of former prosperity, and her old homes reflect a worthy past that bequeathed personality to the present.

Most valid of Milan's claims to distinction is the fact that here was born the greatest scientific inventor of the present age, Thomas Alva Edison. To be sure, he lived here only a few years during his early boyhood, yet his birth on February 11, 1847, in the little red-brick cottage at the northern edge of town, overlooking the valley, sheds glory sufficient for any town.

The Edison Cottage possesses little of architectural interest. It was just a comfortable home for a family of modest means in a pioneer community (Plate 193). The interior woodwork is simple and of the kind that was worked out commonly by the village carpenters of the time. The date of its erection is uncertain and its history uneventful except for association with this one little boy.

PLATE 193: *Birthplace of Thomas A. Edison, Milan*

Quite outstanding in dignity and character is the Mitchell-Turner House, a classic structure distinguished by a pediment supported by Ionic columns, and with a wing on each side. The general effect is impressive, and an air of richness is added by the ornament on pediment and doorway. This consists of sawed and applied fret, the design of which follows closely the lines of classic ornament, the two bands of ornament on the doorway being especially good.

Little definite information is available regarding its history, except that it was built about 1828 by a man named M. Mitchell who was both owner and builder. The lumber used in its construction was native whitewood and black walnut. It is unfortunate that so little is known of this builder, for his handling of details indicates that he was a person not only of fine taste but having exceptional understanding of architecture. We may well assume that he was the possessor of books on classic architecture, from which he studied his ornamental design, for it is too accurately rendered to have been produced by one who merely remembered it from apprentice or college days.

JEFFERSON, ASHTABULA COUNTY

The fourth town of this historic quartette is Jefferson. Its broad, beautifully shaded streets are still faced by old houses that are worthy of consideration here, but the personalities associated with them in the past give to the place greater distinction than comes from its architecture.

The earliest settlement was made here in 1805, and it was made county seat through the efforts of Gideon Granger by whom it was named after Thomas Jefferson, under whose administration Granger had been Postmaster General of the United States. Platt R. Spencer, who developed the Spencerian system of penmanship, spent a portion of his boyhood here, and the family of William Dean Howells lived here, his father and brothers editing the *Ashtabula Sentinel,* oldest newspaper in the county and one that is still in existence.

PLATE 194: *Mitchell-Turner House at Milan*

The most distinguished citizens of this little county seat were Benjamin F. Wade and Joshua R. Giddings. Both were successful lawyers, and were partners for many years; both were for long periods members of Congress, where they were fearless and outspoken advocates of abolition. Wade was acting Vice President of the United States under Johnson, and had one more senator voted for Johnson's impeachment, Benjamin F. Wade would have replaced him as President. Giddings' record may best be told briefly in the words inscribed on a bronze tablet attached to a great boulder that stands in front of his old law office:

"Joshua Reed Giddings here wrote the Republican Party's first national platform, adopted at Philadelphia June 17th, 1856. Member of Congress 1838-1858. In 1842 he defied the Atherton Gag Rule, prohibiting discussion of slavery on the floor. Censured by the House, given no opportunity for defense, he resigned. His overwhelming reëlection five weeks later, and renewed defiance, restored constitutional freedom of speech in our American Congress.

"Pioneer soldier, author, patriot and statesman.

A founder of the Republican Party."

✶ ✶ ✶ ✶

The law offices of these two distinguished Ohioans still stand, that of Giddings on the original lot beside his old home. The Wade office has been moved a few blocks from his home and placed in a little park. Both are tiny buildings such as many early doctors and lawyers built for themselves (Plates 27, 186 and 196). They are of frame construction and very simple in design. The Giddings office still houses the desk, law library, safe, and other belongings of its illustrious owner. The safe was the first brought to Ashtabula County. This office was built in 1823 and for many years was used jointly by the two lawyers while practicing under the firm name of Giddings and Wade.

The names of Elisha Whittlesey, Benjamin F. Wade, and Joshua R. Giddings may well be associated here, for they had the

PLATE 195: *Doorway at Milan*

[304]

same pioneer background, their careers were closely linked together, and all three were conceded to rank among the greatest lawyers of their time.

Whittlesey's home still stands in Canfield, as does Wade's in Jefferson, but the Giddings home burned many years ago. The Wade House is not of sufficient architectural interest to warrant its publication here, but its historic value may be judged from the legend on a bronze tablet set up in its front yard. This reads:

"Home of Benjamin F. Wade. A vigorous defender of Human Rights. U. S. Senator, 1852-1870. Acting Vice-President under President Andrew Johnson. Had one more senator voted for impeachment, Senator Wade would have become President of the United States.

"Also home of Maj. Gen. James F. Wade, military governor of the Philippines and member of the Cuban Evacuation Commission.

"His son, Maj. Ben Wade was in command of the troops on the *Tuscania* torpedoed off the Irish coast by a German submarine. The last soldier to leave the sinking ship."

Another tablet set up in front of the Congregational Church throws light on other events that have added luster to this town's history. It reads:

"First Woman's Suffrage Convention held in this church in 1844 by Ashtabula County Women's Anti-Slavery Society. John Brown spoke here May 27, 1859."

The original church building has been replaced by a more recent structure of doubtful architectural value, a fate that has befallen altogether too many important buildings throughout the state, but in spite of its losses Jefferson still retains much of the atmosphere that is to be anticipated in a town whose past has been so intimately associated with events and persons of great historic importance.

✓ ✓ ✓ ✓

PLATE 196: *Law office of Joshua R. Giddings, Jefferson. Built in 1823*

In Conclusion

It is a great temptation to expand beyond the confines of these four old towns into other fields where houses, personalities, and historic incident afford enticing material for text and illustrations. Mention might well be accorded Lancaster with its memories of John and William Tecumseh Sherman, of Thomas Ewing and a coterie of famous jurists, together with the fine homes which formed a background for their social life. Chillicothe might be given an entire chapter as the state's first capital and home of many of its early leaders. Fremont is a near neighbor of Norwalk, and the former home of Rutherford B. Hayes. Lebanon claimed Tom Corwin, Zanesville stands at the strategic spot where the National Road crosses the Muskingum River at the head of navigation. It was also the home of an historic glass industry and for two years capital of Ohio.

All of these places still possess many old houses that recall personages who added luster to history, houses that challenge the admiration of architects, and tempt the scholar to delve into local records.

Hudson has been spoken of in connection with its old college; Hiram, Oberlin, and others should have been; the churches of Atwater and Tallmadge have attracted attention to these two little villages; and the latter also deserves mention as an early example of studied town planning, and as the birthplace of Delia Bacon who in later life became famous through her participation in the Shakespeare-Bacon controversy.

However, it seems undesirable to widen the field of this chapter, or of the book; the material available is so great in quantity as to preclude anything like complete or adequate treatment. It seems best merely to choose here and there examples that illustrate types, or that possess peculiar interest. Innumerable photographs have been discarded, and greater numbers of old buildings have been passed by without benefit of camera because of the impossibility of gathering all the fruits of this research.

Much of the state's area has not been touched, in spite of the tens of thousands of miles covered in the quest, and all that has been attempted here has been to suggest in a general way the wide range and high standard of accomplishment which may be accredited to Ohio's pioneer builders.

Mounting Block, Sunbury Tavern

APPENDIX

THE following contracts were entered into between Henry B. Curtis and various contractors who were engaged in building operations on the house in Mount Vernon which is described on page 155. These unusual documents are reproduced by courtesy of Henry C. Devin, grandson of the original owner and the present occupant of the old house.

In a letter which accompanied these contracts, Mr. Devin wrote, "The mantels described in contract No. 9 were for use in the double parlor at the south side of the building. It is interesting to observe the desire or ambition of the owner and builder to secure these marble mantelpieces, which he had the vision to see were the proper thing for the style of room contemplated. The amount of work and trouble it meant to achieve this purpose! John Hunter and Henry Lemmon were English stonecutters who had been brought to Gambier, Ohio, by Bishop Philander Chase for work in construction of the stone building of Kenyon College. They were considered unusually good workmen, and represented that they could do "fine marble work."

The owner was to furnish the necessary "pieces of marble." These were brought to Pittsburgh in some way, thence via the Ohio and Muskingum Rivers to Zanesville. Mr. Curtis then sent his own team and wagon to Zanesville and hauled the marble to Mount Vernon. One of these mantelpieces still stands in the house in a second-floor bedroom (Plate 106).

CONTRACTS

Memorandum of an agreement and Convenant on the part of Westley Irvin and Eliphalet Armstrong to and with Henry B. Curtis—The said Irvin & Armstrong for and in consideration of the covenants of said Curtis hereinafter specified agrees to do all the carpenter and frame work in and about said Curtis new House (now about to be built) so far as all the platforms for the floor and roof, including the roof itself—And it is understood that the said New House for the said Curtis will be fifty three feet by forty two feet, and the construction of the said platforms is to include all Samson girders, joists, ties and supports, by whatsoever name the same may be called, necessary to make the said platforms good, substantial and for receiving neat finish and good work—The joists to be all lined and hewed even on the edges so as to admit of level floors and ceilings without further furrying—And the roof to be framed in a strong and substantial manner, and suitable to the building, having reference to the size of the house and the order and arrangement of the partitions, and consistent with the most approved principles of Architecture.

The said work to be in readiness and carefully and properly placed and secured in their places on and in the wall as the work progresses, without creating any further delay to the Mason work than actually necessary. Also to make and put up in a neat and workmanlike manner a modillion Ionic cornice, horizontal & raking, for the whole house, according to the representation (above the frieze) in plate 55 in Shaw's Architecture, omitting the cutting the bed fillet into small dentals as represented and the square on which said dentals are set—Also the Horizontal part of cornice to be constructed with a frieze and architrave of suitable width and proportion. The Architrave to be as represented in plate 57 of said Shaw's Architecture, omitting the lowest moulding and the square on which it is cut—And the frieze to be made with frets over the windows as constructed in the cornice of Bishop McIlvaine's house at Gambier—Said fret windows not exceeding five in number—It is understood that said Curtis has the privilege of omitting the modilions in the west cornice if he sees proper and in that case there is to be a reduction in the price according to the proportion that the labor is lessened. The said Cornice and its finish to be in a state of forwardness by the time the building is ready to receive it, so that the whole job may be finished with as little delay as practicable the ensuing fall. And the roof to be put on said building without delay after the walls shall be up ready for the same.

And the said Curtis on his part agrees to pay for said work, upon completion of the job as follows: One third in money—One Third in store goods—and one third in good notes, warranted by said Curtis to be collectable—The said goods and notes and money to be paid upon demand after completion of said job—And the amount of said job is to be ascertained by the following named measurement and rates of price—Seventy

five cents per square of 100 feet in each platform—The same for the framing and raising roof, counting the roof as a level platform—That is to say,
omitting in measurement all increases of squares on account of the *pitch*
or *raise* of the same—twenty five dollars for sheeting and shingling the
roof—Sixty two and a half cents per foot for the Modillion cornice without
frieze and architrave, and Eighty one and ¼ cents per foot for that part
which will be finished with the frieze and architrave, subject to a deduction on the west cornice as before mentioned—The said Irvin and Armstrong covenanting to do all the work herein contemplated and specified
to be done in a workmanlike manner—without reference to work custom-
arily done in Mt. Vernon, in particular, but with reference to approved
principles as laid down by the writers on Architecture—It is further specified that when in the construction or raising said platform it becomes necessary or expedient to raise a partition for the support of the same by said
Irvin and Armstrong, then for the framing and erection of such partition
they shall be entitled to the farther pay of fifty cents per square of 100 ft.
in said partition—And said Curtis is to furnish all necessary materials for
all of said work, in due season and from time to time as the work progresses and he receives notice of the want of the same—Said Curtis shall
give said Armstrong & Irvin at least one weeks notice of the time when
the walls would be ready (from time to time) for receiving the platforms—
provided that no damage shall be chargeable against said Curtis if the time
runs longer than such notice, nor shall such deferred time be an excuse to
said Irvin & Armstrong for neglecting to proceed with the erection of the
timbers or work when the wall would actually become ready—And on
the other hand no damage shall be chargeable against Irvin and Armstrong for failure to have the timbers ready in due season when there has
been a neglect to give the required notice. Note—the notes alluded to as
part payment to be on individuals in Knox County. The tenders working
on and about said building in employ of said Curtis at the time of erecting
timbers shall be turned in to assist in raising free of charge to said Irvin and
Armstrong.

Witness our hand and seals May 26, 1834.

Duplicates

WESTLEY IRVIN   (SEAL)
ELIPHALET ARMSTRONG   (SEAL)
HENRY B. CURTIS   (SEAL)

Contract between Nathan King of Gambier and Henry B. Curtis of Mt. Vernon—Said King for and in consideration of the covenants of said Curtis hereinafter specified agrees to do all the plastering to be done in said Curtis' new building in Mt. Vernon including Stucco work— the job to be commenced as early as the other work in said home will permit and finished as fast as practicable thereafter—The said work to be done in first rate workmanlike style, without reference to former work done in Mt. Vernon which it is considered is generally inferior to good work—And the said Curtis agrees to pay for the said job of work so done as aforesaid a price and amount which shall be ascertained by the following rate and computation, all two coat work, whether prepared for papering, for white wash, or finished with one brown and one *hard coat,* Nine Cents per yard —All three coat work the last being a *hard coat,* twelve & ½ cents per square yard—All Stucco Cornice for the parlors and halls of suitable pattern and size as said Curtis shall approve 12½ cents per foot in length— Openings and spaces exclusive—And all other work or modes of finish in the business and occupation of the said King, and which the said Curtis may desire to have done in and about his said house, and not above particularly specified, to be rated in the price thereof according to the above specified prices in proportion to the labor required—The pay to be one half in store goods in Shermans or Rogers Store in Mt. Vernon, or such other store as may be agreed on between the parties—or a part at each—The other half in money—The said Curtis to find all materials and the said King to do all the lathing and find his own attendance.

Witness our hands and seals this 10th day of Dec. 1834.

NATHAN KING   (SEAL)

H. B. CURTIS   (SEAL)

Memorandum of an agreement between Henry B. Curtis of one part and John Johnston Jr. of the other part—The said Second party in consideration of the covenant of said Curtis hereinafter specified agrees to furnish to said Curtis at his building lot opposite his present residence all the building stone that he, said Curtis, shall need or require, the quantity not to be less than one hundred perchs, and with the privilege of extending the same to one hundred and fifty perch—to be delivered between this and the first of March next as far as the amount is ascertained and from time to time thereafter as notice may be given for the same, so as to keep the requisite supply on hand and to prevent delay of said Curtis' work—The stone to be of large heavy building size—larger than usual—a full course of which for the bottom of the foundation to be quarried at least thirty inches wide and not less than eight inches thick. The stone is to be furnished also for cutting and making range work to enable the builders to make as heavy looking work as that in the foundation of the Court House in Mt. Vernon—And said Curtis agrees to pay said Johnston as follows: One Dollar a perch for the stone so delivered as aforesaid, to be measured in the wall, excepting for the face stones of the range and cut stone work that shall be placed above the grade of the pavement, which last mentioned stones are to be calculated at one dollar and twenty-five cents the perch— The perch spoken of throughout this memorandum is (as hath been the custom in Mt. Vernon) sixteen and a half feet long—one foot high—and eighteen inches wide—solid work—openings exclusive—The payment to be due at the end of the job in cash obligations, warranted collectable— Said Johnson has the privilege of receiving such proportion of store pay as he may see proper in lieu of the pay above specified.

It is understood that the wall will be at least two feet thick.

The within contract settled and received infull on both parts, Dec. 8, 1834.

JOHN JOHNSTON
H. B. CURTIS

Settled the amount of stone delivered on the within contract, including all extras—and the full price and sum of the same is fixed at One hundred and twenty seven dollars and fifty cents—Sept. 3, 1834, of which my brother Isaac is entitled to one half.

✓ ✓ ✓ ✓

Memorandum of an agreement between Thomas Lusk of Utica of one part and Henry B. Curtis of Mt. Vernon of the other part—The said Lusk agrees to get out the caps and sills for twenty five windows (including one door which will be about the same width as a window) for said Curtis' new house which he is about building in Mt. Vernon—& deliver the same on or before the 1st of August next to said Curtis at Mt. Vernon finished & in good order. The stone of which the same are to be made to be of corresponding color and quality with those used by Dr. Fuller in the front of his house in Utica—It is understood that the glass for said Curtis' windows will be 13 by 20 inches, & and the said caps are to be cut of the following form according to the proportions and pattern that said Curtis may direct—Also the same, together with side pieces for the center front door which will be about nine and a half feet wide (the particular width and pattern to be directed by said Curtis) having in addition to the block at each end a square or Key block represented in the center.

In consideration whereof said Curtis agrees to pay said Lusk at said first of August upon the delivery of the stone work aforesaid, thirty two dollars and fifty cents—And on the first day of December next thirty two dollars & fifty cents—said Lusk agrees to do the said cut stone work in an excellent and workmanlike manner.

Witness our hands this Apl. 28, 1834.

His

THOMAS X LUSK   (SEAL)

Mark

HENRY B. CURTIS   (SEAL)

In consideration that H. B. Curtis agrees to pay to Richard Phillips at the rate of Seventy cents per hundred for good merchantable flooring plank, of ash timber—and at same rate for other poplar stuff not exceeding in all six thousand feet—the poplar stuff of whatever dimensions to be calculated as inch. Therefore I agree to deliver to said Curtis in good seasoned condition the above named lumber from time to time between this and the time of finishing the contemplated new house—he giving me reasonable notice—and a bill or specification of the sizes.—Aug. 20, 1833.

RICH. PHILLIPS   (SEAL)

For value received, I hereby promise to deliver to Henry B. Curtis at or near his building lot opposite his present residence in Mt. Vernon, to be stacked up in good order—ten thousand feet of clean yellow poplar stuff well seasoned, fit for inside work—calculated as in inch measure—to be delivered in such proportions of $\frac{3}{4}$—1—1 $\frac{1}{4}$—1 $\frac{1}{2}$ and 2 inch stuff as said Curtis may by bill or specification direct—To be delivered from time to time as said Curtis may want the same—The whole lot by the first day of May next.

Witness my hand and seal this 20th day of Aug. 1833.

RICH. PHILLIPS   (SEAL)

Mr. Phillips:

You are hereby requested to furnish me under your Contract as soon as practicable the following seasoned poplar timber:

22 pieces to be sawed 13 inches square at the bottom, 11 at top.

Clean stuff, clear of heart, and clear of cracks, being for columns ten feet long each.*

375 ft. of Scantling 4 by 5 inches
375 ft. " " 4 by 4 "
750 ft. " " 3½ " 3½ sawed of such length as to cut into 2 ft.
                                                                    pieces
625 ft. " " 3 " 3 " " " (without waste.
12 pieces " 3½ " 3½ sawed of 13 ft. long each
12 " " " 3 " 3½ " " "
160 ft. " " 3½ " 8 good clean stuff

Also such quantities and proportions of plank and boards as Mr. Dwyer may specify, and particularly a large quantity of 2 inch stuff.

Jany. 25, 1834.

Henry B. Curtis

Apr. 9, 1834 the following bill
   3000 ft. flooring
   1000 ft. 2 inch
   1000 ft. 1½ "
   1000 ft. inch
    600 ft. ¾ inch
    500 ft. 1¼ inch
Mr. H. Curtis Account

Sept. 9, 1833	1871 ft. one inch	1871
14,	400 do.	400
Nov. 1,	800 ft. weather board ½ inch	400
	1092 ft. one and half inch	1638
7,	782 ft. one and fourth 1¼	977½
	152 Do. one and half 1½	228
	144 Do. 2 inch	288
15,	323 Do. 2 do.	686
	262 Do. 3 by 4 Scantling	262
	384 Do. 4 by 4 do.	512

---

*These were all *yellow* poplar, according to the "specifications," were used for the west double gallery porches, and had an interesting subsequent history.

Dec. 16,	153 Do. 2 inch	316
Jan. 23, 1834	198 Do. 1 inch	198
	400 Do. 1 inch	400
May 21,	1375 Do. 1	1375
22,	384 3½ by 3½ Scantling	384
	225 3½ by 3½	225
	138 3½ by 3	127
	450 3½ by 3½	450
31,	360 5 by 4	600
	360 4 by 4	480
	60 3½ by 3½	60
	430 3 by 3	322½
June 21,	80 3 by 2½	50
	388 ft. ¾ inch	291
	1000 ft. 1 inch	1000
	300 ft. weather board ½ inch.	150
July 28,	2000 ft. 2 inch	4000
	1500 ft. 1½ inch	2250
August 1,	1500 ft. 1 inch floorboard	1500
21,	562 ft. 1 inch	560
	160 ft. 4 by 8	426⅔
	22 post 11 ft. long 13 by 11	2883 5/6

Stacking the Board
Kill drying
Mr. Dwins 1000 ft. weatherboards

	500	
	———	
	25802	180.60
17½ cts. added on the hundred of		1.12
2100 ft. ½ inch, if I allow something for		3.67
drying etc.		———
		185.39
		7.00
		———
		192.39

Delivered at Irvins
64 ft. 1¼ inch
97 " 1½

✔ ✔ ✔ ✔

Memorandum—

James S. Fletcher agrees to Dig & wall for H. B. Curtis on his lot opposite his present residence (at such place as said Curtis shall desire) a good well, with durable and permanent water—to commence, provided his health permit, as soon as he shall complete his fall Seeding which will not be more than 2 weeks from this time, and to finish digging and walling up said well as soon thereafter as practicable—Said Curtis to find the stone—the well hole after walling to be three feet diameter—The wall to be good and substantial—And said Curtis agrees to find all necessary tenders after getting below 8 or 10 feet—Also to keep the grubbing hoe (which said Fletcher is to find) in good order—And to pay when the job is finished, one fourth in money, and three fourths in store goods, on demand, a sum which shall be calculated by the following rates—fifty cents per foot for the first twenty five feet—seventy five cents per foot for the next five and one dollar per foot for the remaining part of said well—but if in digging said Fletcher comes into rock digging sooner than twenty five feet then the seventy five cents per foot to commence from that point. Oct. 4, 1834.

JAMES S. FLETCHER (SEAL)
HENRY B. CURTIS (SEAL)

An agreement between John DeWolf, Lloyd McDonald and James Colville, of one part and Henry B. Curtis of the other part—Said first party in consideration of the promises of said Curtis hereafter specified— agrees to deliver flag stone suitable for cutting, enough for making the entire pavement to the front of said Curtis' house and lot in Mt. Vernon, and on the south side the extent of his house and porch—of the following dimensions—The front pavement to be in three courses, which will require stone of two feet 2 inches wide—and to be at least three feet long— The remainder may be in pieces not less than eighteen inches wide and from two ½ to four feet long—not less than five inches thick, and from that to six inches thick (after being dressed)—To be delivered at said Curtis' house in Mt. Vernon, and measured after the same are dressed ready for laying—Said stone to be got out and delivered as fast as practicable and without delay of other work or jobs—So as to enable said Curtis to finish his job of paving before the frosty or rainy weather comes on.

And said Curtis on his part agrees to pay for said stone when so measured as aforesaid three dollars per perch counting twenty five cubic feet to the perch—One third in money, one third in grain and one third in store goods. Witness our hands and seals Sept. 5, 1837.

LLOYD McDONALD	(SEAL)
JAMES COLVILLE	(SEAL)
JOHN DeWOLF	(SEAL)
HENRY B. CURTIS	(SEAL)

Memorandum of an agreement between John Hunter and Henry Lemmon of one part and Henry B. Curtis of the other part—Said Hunter and Lemmon in consideration of the covenants of said Curtis hereinafter specified agrees to make and put up in good City workmanlike manner two fine Marble Mantlepieces with fine polish and glass—of the style, form and manner of the Ionic example on plate 70 in Shaw's Edition of Architecture, Edition of 1831—Subject only to such modifications in size or proportion as may be adapted to the places for which they are intended in the two south parlors of said Curtis' new home in Mt. Vernon, and Curtis approving of such modification—The work to be finished by the 1st of May next, provided the marble be furnished in due time—if any delay takes place in any of the pieces of marble, then reasonable additional time to be given for finishing the job. And said Curtis on his part agrees to pay to Hunter and Lemmon on completion of the job in manner aforesaid the sum of Fifty Dollars, half cash half store goods or grain—and will find and deliver at Gambier the marble out of which he will have said mantles made—And also pay for all iron fastenings necessary in putting the same up. And said Hunter and Lemmon agree to do all the marble work which said Curtis may desire to have done for his own use in and about said house or for his own family purposes—And he is to pay for doing the same in rateable proportion with the above in price and manner, and according the work required on such extra job.

Witness our hands and seals this 19th Dec. 1834. (interlined before signing).

Witness:
   OWEN WILLIAMS

HENRY LEMON	(SEAL)
His	
JOHN X HUNTER	(SEAL)
Mark	
H. B. CURTIS	(SEAL)

BIBLIOGRAPHY

BENJAMIN, ASHER. *The American Builder's Companion; or a System of Architecture Particularly Adapted to the Present Style of Building.* R. P. & C. Williams, 1816; *The Architect, or Complete Builder's Guide.* Benjamin B. Mussey, 1845; *The Architect, or Practical House Carpenter.* Benjamin B. Mussey and Co., 1848.

CLARK, EDNA MARIA. *Ohio Art and Artists.* Garrett and Massie, 1932.

CONOVER, CHARLOTTE REEVE. *Dayton, and Intimate History,*

FORD, JANE COWLES and WHITE, CARRIE HARPER. *Records of the Harper Family.*

FOWLER, O. S. *A Home for All, or The Gravel Wall and Octagon Mode of Building; New, Cheap, Convenient, Superior, and Adapted to Rich and Poor.* Fowler and Wells, 1854.

HOWE, HENRY. *Historical Collections of Ohio.* The State of Ohio, 1907.

KIMBALL, FISKE. *Thomas Jefferson, Architect.* Printed for private distribution. Riverside Press, 1916; *Domestic Architecture of the American Colonies and of the Early Republic.* Charles Scribner's Sons, 1922; *American Architecture.* The Bobbs-Merrill Company, 1928.

KNITTLE, RHEA MANSFIELD. *Early American Glass.* The Century Company, 1927.

LAFEVER, MINARD. *The Modern Builders' Guide.* Henry C. Sleight-Collins & Hannay, 1833; *The Beauties of Modern Architecture.* D. Appleton & Company. 1849.

MAJOR, HOWARD. *The Domestic Architecture of the Early American Republic, The Greek Revival.* J. B. Lippincott Company, 1926.

O'DONNELL, THOMAS E. Various articles in *The Western Architect* and *Architecture.*

PALLADIO, ANDREA. *I Quattro Libri dell' Architettura* di Andrea Palladio. Domenico de Franceschi, 1570.

RANDALL, EMILIUS O. and RYAN, DANIEL J. *History of Ohio, The Rise and Progress of an American State.* The Century History Company, 1912.

SCAMOZZI, OTTAVIO BERTOTTI. *Le Fabbriche e i Disegni di Andrea Palladio.* Giovanni Rossi, 1796.

SHAW, EDWARD. *Civil Architecture: or A Complete Theoretical and Practical System of Building.* Marsh, Capen & Lyon, 1834.

SIPLE, WALTER H. *The Taft Museum.* Bulletin of the Cincinnati Art Museum, January, 1933.

STUDER, JACOB. *Columbus, Ohio; Its History, Resources and Progress.*

UPTON, HARRIET TAYLOR. *History of the Western Reserve.* The Lewis Publishing Company, 1910.

VARIOUS AUTHORS. County Histories.

WING, GEORGE C. *Early Years on the Western Reserve.*

INDEX

A

Adam, Brothers, 29, 33, 127, 133, 215, 235, 244.
Adam design, 33, 57, 291.
Adams-Gray House, cast-iron mantel facings, 23.
Adams, Joel and Joe, 193.
Adams Mills, 23.
Acroteria, 160.
Alcoves, 291.
Allen, Dr. Dudley Peter, 169.
Allen estate, Cleveland Heights, 169.
Allen House, Isaac, 171.
Allen House, Kinsman, 167, 169, 171.
Allen House, Peter, 171.
Allen, Dr. Peter, 169.
Allen mantel, 33.
American Association of Museums, xvi.
"American Builder's Companion" by Asher Benjamin, 135.
American Chemical Society, 61.
"American Domestic Architecture," by Kimball, 295.
American Institute of Architects, xvi.
American Institute of Architects, Cleveland Chapter, xv.
Amherst, 111.
Andrews, S. J., house for, 105.
Angels, specifications revealed by, 43.
Annapolis, Maryland, 129.
Anthemion, 125.
Apartments versus New England houses, 25, 27.
Arches, 291, Arches, Blind, 57; spanning hall, 169; Sustaining, 289.
"The Architect, or Practical House Carpenter," by Asher Benjamin, 121.
Architrave, 237, 243, 244.
Aristocratic life fading, 133.
Ashland, 125.
Ashtabula, 27.

Ashtabula County, 163, 303.
Ashtabula County Women's Anti-Slavery Society, 305.
Ashtabula *Sentinel*, 301.
Astronomical Observatory, third in United States, 53.
Athens, 33.
Athens, Greece, 205.
Athenaeum, Western Reserve College, Hudson, 61.
Atherton Gag Rule, 303.
Atlantic Monthly, 57.
Attempts at classic details, 215.
Atwater church, 41, 135, 188, 307.
Atwater, house at, 149.
Auditor of United States Treasury, 289, 291.
Auditoriums adapted to Mormon ritual, 193.
Aurora, 33.
Aurora, Kennedy House, 135.
Avery, Alfred, 45.
Avery-Downing House, Granville, 45.
Avery, Milan Township, 293.
Avon, Lorain County, 248.

B

Bacon, Delia, 307.
Bacon, Francis R., 236.
Bake-oven, 241, 289; in Brown House, 147.
Baldwin-Buss House, Hudson, 61, 237.
Balusters, 247.
Balustrade, 160.
Banquet hall, Shandy Hall, 165.
Bar, Sunbury, 197.
Barber House, Levi, 113.
Barboursville, Orange County, Virginia, 127.
Barker, Joseph, xv, 90, 111, 113, 115, 117.
Barn, framed with hewn timbers, 202.

[321]

INDEX

INDEX

INDEX

INDEX

INDEX

Tallmadge church, 41, 93, 188; centennial, 41; restoration, 41, 93.

Taverns, 19, 121, 187, 193; Dunham Tavern, 199, 200, 202; Exchange Hotel, 113, 115; Headley Inn, 13, 15; Hopkins House (Sunbury Tavern), 121, 193, 195, 197; Leroy Tavern, 103; Mansion House (St. Charles Hotel), 17, 115; McCartney's Tavern, 25; Mountain House, 103; Old Stone House, 56, 57, 133, 135; Olds' Stage House; 103; Palmyra Hotel, 199; Penn Tavern, 17; Red Brick Tavern, 15, 17; Rider Tavern, 3, 17, 103; Unionville Tavern, 3, 19; Zoar Hotel, 197.

Taylor, Governor, Residence of, 155.

Temple of Concord, Rome, 159.

Temple, Peripteral, 205.

Theseum, 205.

Thompson, Martin E., 207.

Tidewater Virginia, 129.

Tile roofs at Zoar, 199.

Timber, 229.

Timber construction transmuted into marble, 226.

Timbers fastened by wooden pegs, 231.

Treat House, Aurora, 33.

Trumbull County, 149, 169.

Twinsburg church, 188.

U

Unionville, 163.

Unionville Tavern, 19; suggested by Mount Vernon, 3.

Unionville, Warner House, 35, 100.

United States Bank, Cincinnati, 153.

Upjohn, Richard, 211.

Ursaline Convent, Cleveland, 105.

V

Van Buren, Martin, 15, 17.

Vermillion and Vermillion River, 160; Swift House near, 147.

Vermont, 155.

Vernacular, The, 215.

Vicenza, Italy, 127.

Vice President of U. S., Wade as acting, 303.

Victorian carpenters and carpentry, 226.

Virginia, 3, 127, 147; Hardy County, 31; Immigration from, 9; military lands, 7; Poplar Forest, Bedford County, 47.

Virginia and Maryland churches, 129.

Virginia, University of, 47.

Virginians and Marylanders, devotees of soil, 129; took to politics, 187.

Vredenburgh-Gardiner House, Norwalk, 295.

Vredenburgh, John, 295.

W

Wade, Benjamin F., 303.

Wade home in Jefferson, 305.

Wade, General James F., 305.

Wade, Jephtha H., 225.

Wagon wheels frozen in mud, 195.

Wainscoted walls, 239.

Wainscoting, on porch wall, 221; panel to cover oven, 241.

Walker, Thomas U., 211.

Wallpaper, in Brown House, 147; Shandy Hall, 167.

Walpole, Horace, 225.

Walter, Henry, 207, 209.

War of 1812, 97.

Warner House, Unionville, 35, 100.

Warren, 149; Kinsman House, 31, 171; Quinby House, 61, 171.

Washington, George, 3.

Washington Monument Association, 289.

Washington's trail, 9.

Waterbury, Connecticut, 41, 90, 107.

Water wheel, 39, 109.

Watson, Stanley, 15.

Waverly, 151.

Webb, Adaline E., xiv.

West, William Russell, 209.

Welford's, 23.